Testimonial for Cheryl Pasieka

Cheryl is a remarkable person who has embraced her past struggles with unwavering courage and resilience, using them as stepping stones to personal growth and transformation. Through her steadfast commitment to her recovery, she has become a beacon of hope and inspiration for those who are still navigating their own paths to healing.

What sets Cheryl apart is her genuine desire to share her life's lessons with others. She fearlessly opens up about her past, offering a raw and honest account of her journey. By sharing her vulnerabilities and triumphs, she creates a safe space for others to do the same, fostering a sense of community and support.

Through her words and actions, she demonstrates that recovery is not just about overcoming addiction; it is about embracing a new way of life.

I wholeheartedly recommend her as a source of inspiration and support for anyone seeking their own path to recovery and self-discovery.

Meghan Weir
Spiritual & Business Catalyst
Rapid Resolution & Hypnotherapist

Climbing the Stairs

MY JOURNEY FROM ADDICTION TO PURE JOY

Cheryl A. Pasieka

◆ FriesenPress

One Printers Way
Altona, MB R0G 0B0
Canada

www.friesenpress.com

Copyright © 2024 by Cheryl A. Pasieka
First Edition — 2024

All rights reserved.

No part of this publication may be reproduced in any form, or by any means, electronic or mechanical, including photocopying, recording, or any information browsing, storage, or retrieval system, without permission in writing from FriesenPress.

ISBN
978-1-03-830143-7 (Hardcover)
978-1-03-830142-0 (Paperback)
978-1-03-830144-4 (eBook)

1. SELF-HELP, SUBSTANCE ABUSE & ADDICTIONS

Distributed to the trade by The Ingram Book Company

Disclaimer

This book is not intended to be a substitute for the advice of a medical doctor or a mental health professional. The views and experiences described in this publication are the author's personal thoughts and opinions. They are not meant as a definable set of instructions for recovery.

Written in loving memory of
Dad & Mom
who are always with me in spirit

Table of Contents

Introduction 1

The First Stair:
The Decision to Seek Help 7

The Second Stair:
Arrival at the Treatment Centre 15

The Third Stair:
Life in Rehabilitation 21

The Fourth Stair:
Adjusting at Home 39

The Fifth Stair:
New Lessons 49

The Sixth Stair:
Exploring Options. 59

The Seventh Stair:
Expanding My Understanding 67

The Eighth Stair:
Celebrate! 73

The Ninth Stair:
Mindfulness & Positivity. 83

The Tenth Stair:
Connection & Gratitude. 93

The Eleventh Stair:
Giving Back 111

The Twelfth Stair:
Focus & Curiosity. 119

The Thirteenth Stair:
Trusting Your Instincts 131

The Fourteenth Stair:
Tripping on a Stair 139

The Fifteenth Stair:
The Art of Journaling(According to Me!). 151

The Sixteenth Stair:
Food for Thought 159

The Seventeenth Stair:
Secret Medicines & Miracles. 169

The Eighteenth Stair:
...and Still Climbing. 185

Resources 191

Reference. 195

Acknowledgements 197

Introduction

One day you will tell your story of how you overcame what you went through, and it will be someone else's survival guide.

—Brené Brown, American Researcher

My name is Cheryl, and I am a proud recovering alcoholic. This book is about both my approach to sobriety and how I live my life now. I sincerely thank you for reaching out and taking the time to read this. For those suffering from addiction to alcohol, drugs, gambling, eating disorders, sexual addiction, shopping, etc., this book is for you.

This book is also for those who may not have an addiction but are "stuck" in a life that is not bringing great happiness or joy.

We only live once in human form on this earth, so I say, regardless of when you start this journey, there is always time to learn to approach your days and dreams differently.

The year 2020 was a life-changing year for me, as it was for many. At the start of the year, my mom died at ninety-one years of age. We had had a difficult relationship for many years, but I had come to a place of forgiveness and understanding that created a wonderful, new relationship. In her final years, she developed dementia, and it was so difficult to watch her fade away. I looked forward to seeing her every few months at her home in Ontario, but each time, I was reminded that my mom was losing her joy and her memories. The last time we were together, she was crying as I was leaving, and she said to me that it was too hard for her to live now. She also said as she hugged me hard, "I won't see you again. I just know it."

At times, her dementia caused her to question where she was and who others were, and to argue that some of her memories were not true. At other times, she seemed quite lucid, and on that final day, that is how she seemed. It was as if she knew that she truly wouldn't see me again on this earth. It also struck me that she knew the end was near, and she was telling me it was okay because she was tired. It was indeed the last time I saw her. Her death hit me hard because there had been so many years earlier in my life that were filled with blaming, ignoring reality, and not really communicating with her. I wanted more honest and real conversations with her, and it was no longer possible. I was very sad and unable to express it.

A couple of months later, Covid spread rapidly throughout the world, and we began to realize that life might not look the same ever again. It reminded me of Mom, as she had not seen the real world for a couple of years before her death. As a family, we were grateful that she was not alive to see all the changes in social norms, our working worlds, and how we would do life moving forward. It would have been too much for her to comprehend.

But for me, there was another change in store that would affect the rest of my days. In early July of that year, I knew I had to go to addiction rehabilitation. I had been struggling with alcohol for some time, and being housebound with the Covid restrictions certainly did not help. In fact, the boredom allowed me much more free time to indulge. On and off throughout my life I have turned to alcohol in times of stress, depression, and anxiousness. Then I would get back on track and life would continue. This time was different. I tried to stop on my own and, quite frankly, it didn't work.

There was a day in early July of 2020 that upon awakening, I felt different. I had been dreaming that night, and when I woke up, I distinctly remember thinking that this was it ... it was time to stop drinking. I know now that many make this decision after hitting rock bottom. Perhaps an incident that "woke them up" to making changes in their lives. There was not a specific incident. It had been building in my mind for some time that I was on a dangerous path for both my physical and mental health. Being in my mid-sixties, I was seeing that life was short, and it was long overdue to explore the reasons why I drank to excess. It was time to find the root causes. It was time to put excuses into the past and not use them as a crutch anymore. I no longer wanted to waste my days drinking and making

INTRODUCTION

excuses to not participate in life with others. It was also time to live my life more fully, more mindfully, and to stop pretending that all was well. I had lived through two failed relationships, and was now married to my true love, and I didn't want to mess that up.

During the course of the next week, I started researching addiction centres. Within a few days, I had a difficult conversation with my beloved husband to share my research and get his valued opinion on the options and how they might affect our relationship, our lives, and our dreams.

My purpose in writing a story about this chapter of my life and my climb out of addiction is to inspire others who are struggling to find a new path in life filled with joy. One of those barriers for me was my alcohol addiction, and I wanted to learn to be free of the masks I wore. I saw my journey as a very steep set of stairs. Some of the stairs were so steep, especially during my time in a rehabilitation centre, that I pictured a ladder next to the stair. The ladder rungs represented the baby steps to get up to the next level. It was at times very difficult, but I was determined to live out my days with more happiness and joy and free of toxic relationships.

That being said, my story is not just about my journey to conquer my addiction. It is also a story of living differently: living with joy in my heart, and living peacefully. I knew deep in my soul that I wanted to live differently for the remainder of my life.

I want to emphasize that building a different approach to the rest of your life is tough; it is hard work and requires perseverance and dedication. At times, giving up on this dream would have been easy, but I continued to dig deep, and was not going to give up.

This was the most challenging time of my days on earth so far. I hope that those reading these pages will be inspired to reach out for help and for true happiness and peace. If addiction is not an issue for you, I am confident you will find in these pages a way, or perhaps several ways, to live your life more fully and mindfully.

It seems to me that the world is a bit scary these days. However, it has been scary in other generations as well. My parents lived through the Great Depression. My grandfather fought in WWI. My father went to war for his country in WWII. My paternal grandparents moved to a new country from overseas and started a new life with a quarter section of land in the Prairies. So, yes we are concerned for our world and what is going to happen to the planet, but remember that past generations had trying times as well.

Today, I am a very different person than I was a few years ago, and I want to share my joy with the world. I no longer want to live my life "small". I no longer want to do things simply because that is what others in the world expect me to do. I am no longer trying to fit it, but rather I am living as I want with joy, mindfulness, and gratitude. I no longer want to give nourishment to toxic relationships. I want my light to burn brightly and to live in my own truth. I am daring to do it my way: dressing my way, expressing myself my way, following my intuition, and speaking my truth.

The quote at the start of this introduction is written by Brené Brown, an amazing woman, researcher, writer, and speaker. I saw this quote after returning from the rehabilitation centre, and it spoke to me. I was not sure why at that point, but I knew it was for me. I took a photo of it and hung it on my bulletin board in my study. I wasn't sure how it would manifest itself, but knew it was an important piece of my future.

There are many pathways towards a healthier and more fulfilling life.

This was and is mine.

THE FIRST STAIR: THE DECISION TO SEEK HELP

Owning our story can be hard, but not nearly as difficult as spending our lives running from it. Embracing our vulnerabilities is risky, but not nearly as dangerous as giving up on love and belonging and joy—the experiences that make us the most vulnerable. Only when we are brave enough to explore the darkness will we discover the infinite power of our light.

—Brené Brown, American Researcher

On that first day of knowing that it was time, I started some research. I knew of several people who attended Alcoholics Anonymous (AA) in their community and briefly thought that could be an avenue to take. *Just look up a meeting, Cheryl, and go!* However, knowing myself fairly well in terms of follow through, I knew that I needed to be away from distractions to make this work. I knew that I would need support, at times gentle pushing, and at times some tough love. I knew deep down that attending a day program in my home city would not be enough and probably would not be lasting. Through my research, there were no residential treatment centres in my city and, being honest with myself, that's what I needed.

But there was the phase of "pretending". I love to read and have a couple of favourite bookstores. I found myself several times browsing the self-help section or the women's study sections looking for a miracle answer. You know, "Read this book, and all will resolve itself." I suppose what I was looking for was a book by a woman who had wanted change, and the how-to guide of how she did that. I had bought a few of these books over time, and although interesting, they weren't enough to get me to complete sobriety. I remember picking up books on addiction, a couple of times, and implying to the clerk I was buying them as research for "my practice". After all, I wasn't "that addicted."

Being truthful with myself, however, I knew that my addiction was deep and that my will power was not. I had, on many occasions, tried to stop completely. It never worked. In part, it didn't work as the detox was so difficult and painful that it was, quite frankly, easier to give up. As I would find out later, it doesn't work if you are not understanding why you turn to an addiction to mask the pain. It doesn't work unless you have a good plan in place to ensure your success and not repeat your old habits in times of struggle. And finally, it doesn't work until you are 110% committed to doing the work.

I read about different treatment centres and their approaches, and I knew that I needed supervised detox. I also was very aware of the fact that unless I started to understand my addiction through intensive therapy that I would be on a merry-go-round. Without that deep understanding and acceptance, I knew I was destined for failure. I knew deep down that until I brought to light incidents of my past, dealt with them, and finally let them go, that I would not be successful. I wanted to climb the stairs, one step at a time, taking whatever time I needed to make sure this was going to work once and for all.

I found a centre that sounded like a fit for me. The centre that resonated with me, at least reading the website, was located on Vancouver Island. I knew in my head that this was what I needed to do, but like any major decision, I was flip-flopping back and forth as to whether I really needed to do this. I had done the research. I had shared it with my husband, but I couldn't seem to actually pick up the phone. There was even a place on the website to leave contact information, and they would call you. If I did that, they might call at an inconvenient time, I told myself. Did I honestly think they would call in the middle of the night? It actually occurred to me that they might call too early in the morning, and I would still be asleep from too much alcohol the day before. Or perhaps deep in my mind, I was afraid they would call when I had had a few drinks. Is that what was inconvenient, Cheryl?

For a number of days, I procrastinated with these thoughts in my mind. The hours and days were ticking onwards. I recalled a book I had read many years ago called *Feel the Fear—and Do it Anyway*. The problem was that yes, I was feeling the fear, but I couldn't seem to muster up the "do it" part. A couple of times, I actually picked up the phone, but was paralyzed to dial the number. That then became picking up the phone, dialing the number, and then hanging up. I remember thinking, *Well, at least I am making progress!*

Throughout that procrastination period, I kept coming back to asking myself to be brutally honest about my addiction. When I was honest with myself, I knew there was no other avenue to take.

It took me about ten days or so to actually allow the call to go through to an addiction centre called Cedars at Cobble Hill, Vancouver Island. I spoke with the Director of Admissions, a gentleman named Ethan. I was unsure what to expect on this initial call, and quite frankly I was scared, as well as embarrassed about my situation. But then I told myself that being embarrassed was ridiculous: as if the Director of Admissions was not used to these types of calls! As it turned out Ethan was compassionate and gentle. His questions were non-judgemental, and he was easy to talk to. Even when he asked the tough questions, I felt safe and at ease in honestly sharing my story with him. The support I felt was strong, and I knew in my gut that this was the place. This was the time.

Perhaps, it was another small piece of procrastination, but I asked to have approximately two weeks before flying out. I wanted time to put my affairs in order. I wanted time for my husband, Roger, and I to adjust to the decision. Also, I needed time to figure out if and how to tell my family. Who would I tell, and who wouldn't I share it with? I also wanted time to decide whether I would tell anyone outside of the family that this was happening. In retrospect, it was another stall tactic, but I did go ahead and book a non-refundable flight.

I knew that if the roles were reversed, although I would be taken back a bit by hearing this news from a family member, I would be there cheering them on. However, I wasn't sure if this would happen to me. In the end, I only told my daughters and my brother. If I am honest with myself, I was not 100% sure I would get a cheerleader reaction from my siblings. Based on what you ask? No idea, just a feeling. I remember thinking that I wouldn't call my sisters as one had a demanding job, and the other was busy raising her children. Lame reasons you could say, but deep down perhaps, I just wasn't confident I would get support. It had nothing to do with who they were, but rather it was emotionally draining to share with people, and I was exhausted.

We decided to also tell my husband's two children, as we lived close to them, and there would be no hiding from the fact that I wasn't home. After all, I would be attending for a minimum of sixty days. I told Roger that if he needed to share with others as time went on, that that was his call, and I was fine with that. I didn't want him to be in the awkward position of having to make up a reason for my "disappearance". Nor did I want to put him in the position of having to lie to family should they call the house. As it turned out, there were no phone calls anyway.

I was very surprised at the support I got from those with whom I did share. What was I expecting? I don't know—perhaps judgement, sarcasm, backing away, and even losing people from my life. Well, none of the above happened, and that was a huge relief. I was relieved that I could go away for treatment and not have to worry about what others thought. Worrying about what others think of me has been a large part of my life, and getting over this became a goal of mine later in my recovery. Why was I always worried about what others thought of me, including my siblings? Well, as it turned out, I was about to find out!

So, with a flight booked, and the arrival date at the centre set, I was feeling great relief and calm in a strange way. Yes, I was very nervous, but another part of me was "excited" to be rid of this affliction that had weighed upon me for years.

Over the years, I have journaled, but I had not for quite some time. I had a beautiful leather journal that my youngest daughter had bought me on a trip to Venice, and I knew this was the one to bring. Just before I packed it, I wrote on the first page:

A New Journey—Probably the hardest one I will ever take.

Roger was very quiet while driving me to the airport, but he was extremely supportive of my doing what I needed to do. It took me off guard when we said our goodbyes at the airport as his eyes were filled with tears. I was deeply moved and knew that my decision was the right one. He and I had been together since 2009 and married since 2014. This relationship is the best I have ever been in, and I wasn't going to let my disease ruin it anymore.

The Second Stair: Arrival at the Treatment Centre

*True Courage is not the absence of fear,
but rather the willingness to walk through it.*

—Author Unknown

arrived mid-day in Victoria and was picked up by one of the workers who would drive me for the one-and-a-half hour drive to the centre. My head was spinning with that old voice in the back of my head: *You are not worthy. You can't achieve this. This will be too hard. I want to go home.* This was followed by: *You can do this. I am determined to make this work. You are worthy,* and on and on. I was literally shaking in-between thoughts of how I could get out of the car and go home. My escort was very cheerful and talkative, telling me all about the sights along the way. It was very sweet and kind of her, but it was very hard to carry on a conversation not knowing what I could expect over the next two months. Honestly, I don't really remember much of that drive.

Upon arrival, I was greeted by the admissions team and spent an hour with an intake person, clarifying my medical history, my addiction history, and generally getting to know how things would work. Having had several conversations with Ethan before I arrived, I surprisingly felt comfortable and fairly relaxed.

I knew that many of the staff were past addicts or alcoholics and, therefore, there was no judgment. In fact, the young man doing my intake told me his addiction story, which included his brother passing away of an overdose in front of him. The story was horrendous to me, and I felt somewhat safe describing my addiction habits, as my story was tame in comparison. At that point in my sheltered life, I had never really known anyone personally who had been affected by the addiction world. I count my blessings on that issue. Little did I know, but my education was about to expand exponentially.

I would learn as time went on that our stories as addicted people were all tough in their own way. I heard stories of childhood abuse and physical and mental violence, as well as of people living on the street or in shelters, running for their lives, dealing drugs, prostituting themselves for their habit and, of course, many stories of death. I met people who recalled "raising" their siblings due to the addiction of the adults in their house. I met a young woman who told the story of stealing food at the corner store to feed her brother as her mother was unable to care for them. She was five, and he was three.

I realized very quickly that I had been living a life in a bubble. Some of the stories I heard were things I only knew of through television series, movies, social media, and the local news, which was constantly relaying statistics of addiction-related deaths. I also heard about the mental health crises in our provinces and the lack of facilities and funding for those who need help. I was beginning to feel grateful for my past, even though it had its own share of difficult times.

Before giving up my phone, I was able to call Roger to tell him I had arrived safely and not to worry about me. I then read two last texts from each of my daughters, which inspired me. One daughter wrote: "Mom, I am so proud of you to do this…" and the other daughter said: "Take advantage of everything that is offered, and don't give up or run away when things get tough." Those two statements from my girls meant the world to me, and when times were hard during my stay, I reflected back on them. Thank you both.

I was shown to my room and, feeling overwhelmed, I decided a nap was in order. My suitcase and personal effects were still in administration for inspection. Not only did this include the obvious (drugs, alcohol, or food items) but also weapons or items that could be used as weapons. When this came up, I thought that these questions would be for someone entering jail, and I wondered what else I was in for. For some, gone were any skimpy or provocative clothing or t-shirts depicting a darker world. No phones or other electronics were allowed either. For me, being from an earlier generation than most, the lack of electronics was not at all an issue, but I saw plenty of panic in those from the younger generation about the phone issue.

I met with the medical staff, who explained the detox process for someone like myself whose poison was alcohol. It took a few days for this detox to do its work, and after that, I was expected to participate in all activities. There were no exceptions. You can't go to a treatment centre and pick and choose what you would like to do. You are there to work, and my frame of mind at the time was a big YES. I was willing and motivated to participate in all aspects of the treatment.

As someone who thrives on routine and order, a lot of the rules and regulations were not difficult for me to adjust to. I saw many people struggle with the strict routine and the "no exception rules". I supposed that this would be a bit of an adjustment if you had been living on the street or in a dysfunctional home where there were no expectations or rules to live by. For some it was an adjustment just being required to make their bed every morning, let alone have it inspected afterwards! We were also expected to eat healthy food at specific times, drink no more than two sugar drinks a day, attend everything on our treatment schedule, and participate in the activities that went on until 9:00 p.m.

Personally, being retired, if I don't want to do something at home, I can simply change my mind and perhaps watch a little TV. Not here! The women's lodge had a TV, yes, but there were only certain times it could be viewed, and all wanting to partake had to come to a consensus on what to watch. Needless to say, as one of the older residents, I don't recall ever watching any TV.

During that first two days of detoxing, I explored the facility grounds. It was beautiful. I was on Vancouver Island, which I have always loved, surrounded by beautiful forests and walking trails. I remember picking and consuming blackberries, which don't grow in my province. The facility itself was a series of log cabins, some for women and some for men. At the time I was there, there were more men than women, and more affected by the drug world than the alcohol world.

I felt comfortable. I felt safe. Let the work begin!

The Third Stair: Life in Rehabilitation

There are only two days in the year that nothing can be done. One is called yesterday and the other is called tomorrow, so today is the right day to love, believe, do, and mostly live.

—Dalai Lama

It was at the treatment centre that I attended my first Alcoholics Anonymous/Narcotics Anonymous (AA/NA) meeting. I didn't know anyone who had ever gone to treatment or recovery meetings, so I really had no idea what to expect. I walked in the lecture hall, and the chairs were arranged in a huge circle. It was the first time I realized just how many people were at the centre, and it was overwhelming. At this stage I really hadn't met anyone.

I quickly realized I was expected to talk in front of these strangers, and I felt sick to my stomach. This was the first time I wanted to "run". I went to the washroom during the meeting, with a half attempt to leave afterwards. Then I chatted with myself: *You are not here for a vacation, Cheryl. You are here to participate in ALL the tools offered and to work hard. Period.* So, back to the group I went.

While listening to other brave souls standing and speaking, it dawned on me that it would soon be my turn. I would have to stand in front of these strangers and state out loud that I was an alcoholic. It became apparent that this was the expectation. That was going to be difficult as I had never said that out loud other than whispering to myself that "maybe" I had an alcohol problem…"maybe".

I soon learned that being an alcoholic or an addict (or both for some) didn't depend on the amount that you consumed. It was the fact that you couldn't take it or leave it. It was the fact that your life was consumed by scheduling around your drinking or your next fix.

I reflected back to the time since my retirement, and realized that I was rising each morning and doing all I had to do outside of my home in the morning only. This would free me up to stay home for the rest of the day and evening and partake. I did not drive drunk, and I was committed to that, but I lived in fear there would be an emergency, and I would have to admit I couldn't drive. Even worse, I was afraid I would someday drive, saying to myself that it would be okay just this once. I drank, although not as heavily, as when I was still out in the workforce. However, I never drank during my work day, nor missed work due to hangovers or such. In retrospect, I suppose that I somehow felt I didn't have a problem since I had never allowed alcohol to interfere with my job.

During week one, I learned about the starting signs of alcoholism and took notes on the progression. This learning session was an eye-opener. I learned that in the real world, for those still denying their addiction, it is very easy to say: "I am not an addict/I am not an alcoholic, as I never passed out, I never drove intoxicated, I never lost a job, I never drank at my job, I was never hospitalized, I don't have an alcoholic diseases," etc., etc. An addict, regardless of the poison, will tend to justify anything to manoeuvre through life.

Here are my notes on the starting signs all the way down to death. Note: These are symptoms, NOT causes. The examples added to the notes are mine, but you may want to consider your own experiences. It is irrelevant where I was on the scale, but I certainly recognized most. The "starting signs to death list" may sound melodramatic, but perhaps take some time to see where you fit in at this point in your life. Be brutally honest with yourself.

Starting Signs of Alcoholism

1. Memory blackouts
2. Urgency, e.g., I need a drink now before company arrives
3. Excuses so you can stay home and continue to drink
4. Persistent remorse, e.g., "Sorry I said that; sorry I did that; sorry, sorry, sorry."
5. Trying to control it, e.g., "I will only drink on weekends.

Okay then, I will only drink three days per week," or "I will only consume two a day." Really, this stage is about playing games with yourself.

6. Self-promises fail: The resolution of not indulging today didn't work; the resolutions of trying to control it are no longer working.

7. Loss of interest: in your job, volunteering, a hobby, your family, and most of all, in yourself. Not wanting to do anything but indulge.

8. Avoidance of situations where you can't drink

9. Loss of willpower to do anything

10. Money troubles: Have you ever calculated how much you are spending on your addiction? I did…scary!

11. Decrease in alcohol tolerance: This is primarily due to liver diseases, which I was told I had. My justification to myself was, "Well, I don't drink as much as I used to."

12. Increased resentment towards others; blaming *them* for the problem

13. Decrease in food consumption, e.g., I had stopped breakfast and lunch—and often beyond that.

14. Decrease in self-care, e.g., no makeup, not getting dressed, lack of hygiene (I'll shower tomorrow)

15. Pain—both physical and emotional

16. Increased anxiety, fear, depression, self-isolation, suicidal thoughts

And then there is rock bottom:

17. Alcoholic seizures

18. Feeling sick, but drinking anyway to feel better

19. Suicide/death

Where was I on the above list you ask? To be completely transparent, I did not experience seizures, suicide attempts, or death. I could relate, in varying degrees, to the rest of the list.

Another regular meeting at the treatment centre was called "The Big Book" study. The Big Book was written by AA and comprised a series of real-life stories about addiction and healing. Each meeting consisted of reading a chapter out loud in a small group, followed by having a discussion about the story. Think of it as an "Alcohol/Narcotic Book Club".

At the same time, with the guidance of my individual counsellor, I started working on the Twelve Steps and the Twelve Traditions. I wasn't sure about these steps. I was raised going to church and Sunday school, but that had stopped as an adult. I would say that I am spiritual, believing in something greater than me, but I am not sure about organized religion. I remember hearing many times in my life, including from my father, that being spiritual is not what you do at the church building on Sunday mornings. Being spiritual is what you do each and every day as you manoeuvre through life.

The language of the AA/NA steps seemed outdated, and I felt some discomfort with the process. However, I went along with the methodology knowing that I didn't need to understand the reasons, but rather needed to trust the process. After all, they were the experts. It wasn't until later when I was home that I realized that there were other options out there to consider, which I will touch on later.

One of the most interesting people I met was a gentleman named Bruce, who was Metis and the spiritual leader at Cedars. I had no background at all with Indigenous traditions, so I was fascinated in rituals such as smudging, which we could participate in several times daily.

Bruce was a kind, gentle man. Aside from the smudging, I was introduced to another Indigenous tradition called a burning ceremony. The purpose of the burning ceremony is to let go of past hurts and anger that are still raging in your body. To start with, I was told to write a letter to a person that I was struggling with. In my case, this was a family member. The issue kept creeping into my daily thoughts and my life and, therefore, obviously I had not let it go.

It was not required to send the letter to the person, or even discuss it with them if I chose not to. I wrote pages and pages about the issue (this is called a "shame/resentment letter") to this particular family member with whom I was struggling. The letter was in great detail, and it took some time to compose along with many tears. After a few days of composing the shame letter, I was then able to invite two individuals to witness my ceremony, which would be conducted by the elder. I chose two members of my small group therapy sessions: Lindsay and Dave.

A roaring fire was going outside a sweat lodge. We stood with our backs to the fire and positioned ourselves at each point of a compass. We were told to study the sky. The day was partly cloudy, and each of us was asked to describe what we saw in the clouds in our direction. For example, one participant saw an eagle shape in the clouds above.

After we all participated, we then turned and faced the flames. For a short period, we just watched the dancing of the flames, and then I was to read the letter out loud to my witnesses, supervised by the spiritual leader, Bruce. I was certainly choked up with tears and found it difficult to read the details of the letter. Then Bruce asked me to put each page of the letter into the fire, one at a time, as we watched the papers burn and disintegrate. We then all closed our eyes as he recited prayers asking the spirits to take away the shame and resentment that I had been holding on to for years. I can't tell you how powerful and emotional this stage was. I had never in my life felt so moved.

We then were instructed to open our eyes and tell him what we saw in the sky now that we had asked for the shame and resentment to be taken away. I swear to you, the reader, there was not a cloud in the sky. Anywhere. Bruce said that the spirits had listened. I was in awe and a bit frightened. But I was also full of gratitude and felt a tremendous sense of relief. It has been near four years since that day, and I have to say, I no longer dwell on that incident with my family member that happened many years before. When I do, it does not nag at me or take away my energy. I remember the incident and set it aside as a part of my life. Although dramatic at the time, I now simply see the story as a part of my journey.

Another activity based in Indigenous culture was called the "Sacred Circle", which I participated in several times. A Sacred Circle is a traditional symbolic circle that incorporates the spiritual beliefs of many Indigenous tribes in North America. It represents the belief in the infinity of our energies in pursuit of connection, unity, and harmony; life as a sacred circle. There were about ten of us participating each time, and it was facilitated by Bruce, our spiritual leader. In one of the sessions, we each chose a rock from the outside grounds and were asked to study it and express what we saw in the rock. I kept looking at mine, and all I saw was a grey rock, as I shuffled it back and forth in my hands, carefully listening to the other participants. As we heard from each participant around the circle, some people described seeing strength; another saw a small rock, as they too felt small in this world; another saw a shape of an animal's tooth and believed that was powerful as they hoped to regain their power as they now felt they were seen as weak.

I was feeling and seeing nothing, but just before it became my turn, I turned the rock over in my hands and noticed that the flip side of my rock had a white vein in it. The vein appeared to have an outline of a human head, and I felt a strong feeling that this was a bust of my mother. *This is crazy,* I thought, and before describing it to the group, I showed it to Bruce who was sitting next to me and asked what he saw. He replied that it looked like a person's head. I started crying, as I felt my mom's strong presence supporting me. I don't know how else to explain the powerful feelings I felt at that session. I still don't know how else to explain it, but I no longer question it. *It is what it is,* I say to myself, even to this day. The rock is home with me now, and I often pull it out to study it and give thanks to that powerful spiritual day.

I also learned to make a medicine bag from the spiritual leader. We cut out hide, sewed on beads, and made a rope from sinew. To this day, it hangs in my car for protection.

As I described earlier, the everyday routines were strict. There were days that I was exhausted mentally and physically, but no exceptions were made. I realized later that this was, in part, building the muscle for later when I would be home and need tremendous strength to keep going and not relapse. *Keep pushing through,* I kept telling myself. *Trust the process, Cheryl.*

The routines included regular meals. At first, I said, "No, thank you. I don't eat lunch." But there was no such thing. We were building strong habits for the future, and if you couldn't do it at rehab, you likely would not back in the "real" world.

After lunch, there was a daily walk around the beautiful, forested property, and again no exceptions. At first, I didn't understand the significance of routine, but I came to see that many in addiction have no routine in their lives, no purpose. We needed to strongly build this muscle in preparation for going home.

One of the meetings that was most helpful to me personally was my one-on-one with my amazing counsellor, Stephanie. Stephanie was a strong, yet gentle woman who obviously deeply cared for her clients. I had one-on-one meetings with her where we deeply explored the root causes of my depression, masking, and substance use that allowed me to hide from the hurt and not be truthful with myself. I was learning where some of my beliefs came from. Together, over the two months, we explored events that led to a lifetime of feeling shame, resentment, anger, regret, and isolated. I learned that if I continued to hold onto these feelings, eventually I would find myself back where I started. Through my time with my counsellor, I sifted through my past, one thing at a time, and learned to let go. It also became clear how these feelings were manifesting themselves into my life, and I began to see how the events and patterns repeated themselves over and over again.

I was encouraged by the exploration and clues to the life I had been living. Small events in my past were coming back to me, giving me a better understanding about my addiction. As was my nature, I hadn't processed some of these traumas. I had just filed them away and hid from the truths, as it was easier. I was recalling events from way back that I had not realized were still paralyzing me. I often wondered if I had gotten counselling or therapy earlier in my life, would I have averted my eventual addiction? I have no answer for that one.

I also participated in a weekly "small group" meeting with five or six others and our counsellor. I found them the most useful, in part because they were more intimate, and not as intimidating as the evening AA/NA meetings. It was at these gatherings that each of us told our stories, and therefore, we became very close to each other. Some had lifetimes of shocking events; others were traumatized by specific events as a child and/or as an adult. Again, I was grateful for the safe family environment that I grew up in with Mom, Dad, a brother, and two sisters. I knew too, that although it was a safe family compared to others, it was still a family that didn't always communicate with each other when life offered difficult moments. There were things that just didn't get talked about in my childhood home and, for me, that led to even more secrets and dealing with challenges on my own. In time, I saw that my parents had done the best they knew how from their upbringing. I let go of blaming and accepted this, which was a big step for me.

Every week, there were numerous training sessions about various subjects around addiction, starting with the history of Alcoholics Anonymous and Narcotics Anonymous. Some meetings were another participant telling their story of how they got to where they were today. Other times, it was an actual counsellor telling their story of addiction before getting sober/clean and then educating themselves to become a counsellor.

There were also training sessions on coping at home, going back to work, or dealing with family and friends later. It was critical to not put yourself back into the same surroundings and increase the chances of a relapse. If there was no choice on that front, strategies needed to be put into place to increase the chances of success. Many would not go home afterwards, but instead go to a half-way house to reintegrate into life while ensuring that the tools learned were supported. I again was grateful that I was returning directly home to my husband, family, and a few friends who were behind me.

Somewhere around week three, one of the training sessions in particular really resonated with me. The subject was getting rid of resentments and shame. We learned that resentments are the number one threat to serenity and sobriety. This got my attention! I knew I needed to work on every aspect of sobriety, not just the obvious one of "do not indulge in your drug of choice".

There was an interesting lecture about blame. I jotted down notes that suggested, "Yes, that happened to you; yes, that shaped your life; but NOW you have a choice." You can continue to wallow in those past mistakes, the past hurts, or past incidents. Or you can make a choice to do what is right for you now, let go of the energy it takes to keep the past alive, and put that energy into moving forward. Sounded simple enough. Of course it isn't, but I was very encouraged to know that it is possible to heal and move forward.

I spent a lot of time exploring past resentments throughout my life that may have contributed to the building anger that I masked with drink. I learned that holding on to those thoughts can consume you, and when it was too much, guess what I did? Hide, isolate, drink. I knew that I continued to hold onto shameful events throughout my life. I was telling myself that: I am not worthy. I am undeserving of love, even from myself. I am not a good parent. I am not a good friend. I am not a good sister, daughter, and auntie. People keep abandoning me. And on and on it went. I knew in my heart that unless that started changing, I would be back where I started and the circle would continue.

Throughout my adult life, in the "good" times, I did not overindulge. It was more so when a dramatic event happened that I would get out my alcohol crutches; times like going through a divorce, losing a long-term job quite unexpectedly, or experiencing conflict with a friend or family member. There were a number of events like that in my life that I discussed during treatment, but I have chosen not to share them outside of the safety of counselling. We all have had our traumas, some worse than others, and they do not go away naturally. They stay deep in the soul until you deal with them constructively.

After one session, I wrote in my journal: *We tend to strongly condemn in others what we can not admit in ourselves.* Mulling this over and over during and after treatment was an eye-opener to realizing how easily I judge people. I wanted to work on that moving forward. This particularly became relevant later when I started to share with some people where I had been for the entire summer. Although they said the words, "Good for you," I never heard from them again. I assumed it was because they didn't want to associate with a former drunk and really were not the friend that I thought they were. Now when someone shuts me out, I no longer assume it is about me. I tend to think that perhaps something is going on in their world at the moment, and I no longer take on the burden of blaming myself. I have talked to a couple of people who I am convinced started to contemplate their own situation or that of their friends and family around addiction. For myself, I was beginning to reshape my life, and I knew that not everyone would remain in my circle, as I moved on to more self-awareness and joy.

One of the hardest parts of rehab for many, myself included, was that traditionally Sundays were visitor days. As we were in the summer of 2020, Covid was ramping up, and this was cancelled. People with families in the areas, particularly those with children were affected greatly. This obviously added even more stress to being away in rehabilitation.

As I didn't have people in the area, and I lived out of province, this was not as difficult. But what was difficult was that my "family visit" was a fifteen-minute phone call once a week to one person. For the most part, this call was to Roger, although I was able to speak to my two daughters and my brother once or twice. I couldn't call ahead, so I risked that they would answer the phone when I called. Alternately, Roger would arrange the call in advance. It wasn't like I had possession of my cell phone and could text. No, my weekly phone call was made on an old-fashioned, black, telephone-booth phone! I hadn't seen one of those for many years!

Shortly after my arrival, I started participating in a Kundalini yoga class. I had never heard of Kundalini before, nor had I ever done yoga, and I wasn't sure about it. As it turned out, this type of yoga is more about spiritual awakening and awareness than being able to bend like a pretzel. I found I quite enjoyed it, and I did it from a chair (older knees and hips!). A huge shout-out to my teacher, Meghan, who was so encouraging. Little did I realize it at the time, but Kundalini yoga with Meghan as my teacher/supporter/mentor would become a regular part of my journey once I went home (more about that later).

Every day I was learning. I was starting to feel overwhelmed, but at the same time, I knew I was building an incredible "tool kit" to take with me. I was determined to only attend rehabilitation once in my lifetime. I was diligent about learning and about building strength for when I left the sanctuary of a rehabilitation centre.

I met many people who for a variety of reasons had been in a facility like this one several times. It was interesting to me that some were funded to attend through their Indigenous band. Others were funded by the court system (a choice of attending rehabilitation or attending jail); some were funded by their employers' employee assistance programs (EAP); and still others by their parents. I was here on my own dime (well, actually, many, many dimes) and was taken back by the thought that this might not work the first time. This strengthened my determination at the time, and it still does to this day.

I had so much to learn—not just about my recovery, but about the real world in general. I needed to see the world with new "open" eyes and leave the judgements behind. I realized that when you judge others, very often it is because of your lack of knowledge about that person or their culture. For example, all Irish people are drunks; all politicians are corrupt; all Indigenous people are lazy; all men are abusive; all young people are poor communicators, etc. I wanted to open up my views, and I wanted to learn and understand. I wanted to learn more tolerance. The list of learnings was long. Actually, it was *very* long.

I came to the realization that for the first year or so of sobriety I would be focused on remaining sober and learning what worked, or conversely, did not work for me towards that goal. I knew that not everything I was learning would work for everyone, and that my path was up to me. A quote that came up often in training or counselling was: "Take what you need, and leave the rest."

What that meant for me was not dismissing an entire lecture, or an entire culture, or an entire theory by focussing on a part I didn't agree with or buy into. Rather, I was learning and gathering the tools that I felt would work for *my* recovery and letting go of the parts that didn't fit for me. I also wanted to be comfortable about eventually sharing my story with others without shame or regret.

Alcoholic Anonymous meetings and guidelines were one of the areas I wanted to explore more. The original book was written in and around the start of WWII in 1939 and was written for male alcoholics. It was not meant for anyone but the male species. Women were still at home struggling. Or was the thought that women didn't have this problem as they were not under the pressure of being the breadwinner? I never have understood or read anywhere why it was just for men.

There were certainly parts that didn't seem to resonate for me, and perhaps also not for women in general. Therefore, I knew that figuring out *my* journey would be the key for my success. Don't get me wrong: Many, many women that I met and all over the world use the methodology of AA or NA and are very successful. I just wasn't sure it was for me. I knew that if it didn't strongly resonate for me, it was unlikely going to last a lifetime. However, right now I was at a treatment centre, and their teachings would be my approach for now.

The reality was setting in that maintaining sobriety was going to be a tough go, a lot of hard work, and a new way of living. Towards the end of my stay at the treatment centre, training sessions focused on "the real world"—such as the session called "Warnings/Signs of a Relapse". Here are a few questions that I wrote down in my journal because they resonated with me at the time:

- How will I handle triggers that may tempt me to drink?
- How will I handle social situations that include alcohol?
- What will I tell relatives, friends, acquaintances, and neighbours? And to what extent should I share?
- Can I handle alcohol being in my own home?
- How would I handle my spouse having an occasional drink?
- Will I attend AA meetings in my community?
- How much will I participate in the group therapy aftercare?
- What about meditation and Kundalini?
- What happens in a crisis—a difficult event that in the past would lead me back to drinking to push the pain away? How would I now handle it?
- How can I consciously avoid relapse?

The list went on and on…

I worried about these types of subjects, but I was reminded that "one day at a time" was the motto. Some days, you just have to create your own sunshine!

My last ten days or so were spent with my counsellor, Stephanie, building a plan for myself. This planning was critical for when I returned home to my "real life", as I called it—the life that now meant so much more to me than it had in the past. I had survived a few failed relationships, and my rehabilitation was, in part, to ensure I was the best I could be. That meant being able to not only love myself, flaws and all, but also fully enjoying all aspects of my days moving forward. My goal, aside from the obvious one of remaining sober, was to live mindfully and in full appreciation of the gifts I have in my life.

On my final day, my new friend Lindsay was my choice of people to say a few words and present me with my first coin of sobriety. I thought of condensing her words, but with her permission I am leaving nothing out. Thank you, Lindsay, my friend and confidant:

Today, I am honoured to give away my friend Cheryl. She was my first friend in treatment, someone who I trusted with my hurt and with my joy. She is a wise, profound, funny, and truly lovely woman with a charm that is hers alone.

In 1994 she set some awesome goals for her life. She will be resurrecting her definition of success that she wrote so many years ago and living by that definition:

Success is to me:

Approaching every aspect of my life with integrity and commitment, taking ultimate responsibility for my own destiny.

Nurturing my creativity and sharing its joy.

Creating intimacy with all mankind and with nature.

Facing and embracing my fears and taking a risk everyday no matter how small.

Keeping my feeling of security.

In treatment she has rediscovered those ambitions. Her love of her husband, Roger, inspires me. I want to dance like Cheryl. Treatment has brought Cheryl out of her loneliness and back into her dreams of success. We all know that she will work as hard at recovery as she has in treatment.

She then read a beautiful poem written by E.E. Cummings called "I Carry your Heart". Thank you, Lindsay.

I felt confident returning home. I was determined to make this work and find the right path to see that happen. I knew I had to structure my days with new routines and tools. I also knew that Roger would be with me heart and soul. I was blessed that I was returning to my love at home.

I realize that all our journeys are different. Some were returning to a home that was not as safe as mine. Some were returning to loved ones who were not as supportive. Some were going home to be the only one in their home who would be clean and sober. If this resonates with you, part of your work is to fill in the gaps with other types of support—perhaps a local church, an in-person meeting or a meeting online with like-minded folk, or even going to the local library and finding all the meeting schedules for recovery meetings near your home.

We all have our journeys, and I am so very grateful for my supporters. Thank you to all.

After all the goodbyes, I was then off to the airport for the next chapter of my journey.

THE FOURTH STAIR: ADJUSTING AT HOME

Finish every day and be done with it.
You have done what you could.
Some blunders and absurdities,
no doubt, crept in.
Forget them as soon as you can,
tomorrow is a new day;
begin it well and serenely,
with too high a spirit to be cumbered
with your old nonsense.

—Ralph Waldo Emerson

hit my first trigger on my way home. *Boy, that was fast,* I thought. I arrived at the Victoria airport and was struck by how many bars there were in such a small area! I suppose this experience is like when you are watching TV and see lots of advertisements for food and beverages, and suddenly you are looking for snacks!

    I realized for the first time that this was part of what I would be up against at times. This was reality. No longer was I "protected" in the safety of a treatment centre, and it was scary. I was further triggered when on the plane in business class, and the free wine was flowing. It was difficult, I will admit. I wanted to telepathically tell the flight attendant, "Don't you know I just left rehab?" I was drained and anxious and feeling like a fish out of water facing this first challenge by myself. Of the twelve people in this section of the plane, I was the only one drinking a Diet Coke instead of wine. The flight attendant even said, "There is no charge for the wine due to the seat you are in." Thank you…but no, thank you.

    As I stepped into the Edmonton airport, I was relieved to be home, grateful to hold Roger in my arms, and optimistic for my future. When we got back home, Roger told me that he had not been drinking while I was away. At first, I felt guilty for that, as he didn't have an issue with alcohol. However, he said that he was behind me 100%, and there would be no alcohol in the house. He gave it away to family and friends that knew where I was for the summer. Wow, I have never had support like that in my life that I could recall.

    I had many tools to access and a determination that was solid.

I slept well that night (nothing like the comfort of your own bed and surroundings!) and woke in the morning ready for my "daily meditation". I found a series of meditations online (there are many to choose from) that suited me, and I planned this as part of my morning routine. As time went on in my recovery, I discovered that a formal meditation could be substituted with peaceful, silent time and just sitting and being still.

I remembered being told that I needed to not overwhelm myself until the new routines were solid and, therefore, set some simple goals for the first week.

Here is what I had written in my journal:

- Check into local AA/NA meetings dates and times and from that pool of folks, hopefully find myself a sponsor.
- Talk to the treatment centre and get set up on Zoom for recovery and counselling meetings that I will be attending.
- Set up with Meghan, the Kundalini leader, to participate live with her online class, which is two days per week.
- Go for a daily walk.
- Continue to journal daily about my progress, both the positive and negative aspects.

By the end of the first two weeks at home I was into my new routine. I was so grateful for my husband, who supported me all the way. I felt, and still feel, very blessed for that unconditional support.

At the same time, I considered the suggestions from the treatment centre about recovery.

Make no major decisions in the first year.
This includes starting a new major relationship. The focus should be primarily on yourself. Trying to navigate a new partner, which is hard enough to begin with, would likely sabotage recovery. A number of times, people on the group counselling calls I joined talked of wanting to get divorced or starting a new relationship.

Almost every time, the suggestion was to delay until it at least until the first year was under their belt. Off the top of my head, I can think of three new relationships that were tried out by people on these calls, and in every case, they failed. Dealing with the anxiety and heartbreak of a failed relationship can be yet another reason to give up on sobriety.

Take as much time as you are able to adjust to your new life.
This may mean a longer leave of absence from your workplace. This may mean being a homebody while getting into your new routine. This is not the time to look for a new job. This is a time to look after YOU and ensure your health and well-being.

Each day, try to think of one positive thing that happened.
No matter how small, the little things add up and are important. Perhaps list them out on an index card, and when you feel down or are getting nowhere, refer to the list and realize that it may be slow going, but you are making progress.

Continue to try and learn from past mistakes.
This obviously doesn't happen overnight, however, by this point, you have certainly been exploring your past mistakes and starting to identify the patterns that lead you into trouble. Remember to stop fortune-telling about the future. By fortune-telling, I mean dwelling in the unknown, and causing yourselves anxiety over things that may or may not happen. These are the times when your self-talk is telling you that this will never work, you will never get there, or you are not capable.

Personally, I was feeling overwhelmed, but I persevered in mapping out my plan for the next six months. I have always done better at work and home with a concrete plan, a to-do list in a way. The satisfaction of ticking off the boxes each day had worked for me in the past, and I hoped that it would now.

I also wanted to honour myself and ensure success, so decided that I would make a commitment to a few steps at a time, and add to those steps as I was able. *Baby steps,* I reminded myself. Picture a miniature ladder to get to the next stair.

I can't count the number of times that the old negative thoughts entered my mind, playing the old tapes of doubting myself. It can eat you alive, and I was determined to observe the feelings, and let them go. I pictured these negative thoughts like the clouds that disappeared during my burning ceremony at the treatment centre. Another way I picture negativity is like watching the waves of the ocean; as the tide gently flows in, it refreshes you, and as it goes out, it washes the negative thoughts away. I knew for sure that there were going to be some difficult times, but that as I applied some of the tools from my recovery toolkit, they would diminish as time went on. So, I used this energy to build my plan.

My Six-Month Plan

Meetings: I was able to set up the Zoom meetings offered by the treatment centre that I could participate in. AA/NA meetings were held by the alumni every night, and I made a commitment to myself to participate three days per week at a minimum. If I felt I was slipping in any way from my sobriety, I would increase this.

The centre also offered group therapy meetings twice a week. These meetings were particularly helpful as the leader, Jake, got to know everyone's story and was great at assisting with coping tools and suggestions for moving forward. For those who perhaps couldn't afford individual counselling, this was most helpful as there was no added costs for participants.

For at least the time being, I did not seek out local meetings in my community. I felt grateful that these meetings were offered by the treatment centre. If that had not been the case, I know that seeking out local meetings would have been necessary. Bear in mind, as well, that we were only about seven months into Covid at the time, so outside meetings would be virtual anyways and not in-person.

One of the added bonuses of the evening meetings was that almost every meeting, I learned something new. As I have mentioned before, there is an expression in the recovery community: *Take what you need, and leave the rest,* and this works very well.

Listening to another's experience often gave me food for thought. I was on one of the counselling calls with people from the treatment centre and the subject came up about whether or not we had found a sponsor. This is a big "requirement" or "highly suggested" thing in the AA/NA culture, and I wasn't understanding the need. Some on the call had sponsors and talked about the support they received, particularly in "working the steps".

I was challenged by Jake, the counsellor on the call, to explore why I was resistant to finding a sponsor. I needed to explore if I was pre-judging the importance of a sponsor. As was pointed out, I may feel good now, but I haven't grieved the loss (of alcohol) yet, nor had I come close to relapsing or feeling cravings yet. I was advised that it is these times that having a sponsor could be helpful. I understood that a sponsor could help you through one of these challenges. It was this type of new learning that I journaled about, asking myself the hard questions about wether I needed a "coach/sponsor" and being brutally honest with myself about the answers. In the end I did not pursue getting a sponsor knowing that I would be reviewing my plan regularly and could incorporate this into my life at a later date.

Going back to "grieving the loss of alcohol", I realize this may sound odd, but for a recovering alcoholic, it is the time when you are wishing that you could be a "normal" human and consume just one drink occasionally at a special event, like everyone else around you.

Reaching Out: Another suggestion I entered into my plan was reaching out to others. This is not something I do naturally. I spent a career where others reached out to me in my role, not the other way around. I had collected a list of over forty names and phone numbers of other participants at Cedars, the treatment centre. I also had the number for the treatment centre, which I could call 24/7 as there was always a person there to listen. My goal in reaching out was to call at least two people every week and talk about how things were going. For those returning to their community and attending AA/NA meetings, collect those phone numbers from the experienced, seasoned recovering people.

Meditation and Yoga: I committed myself to a daily meditation. In addition, two days per week, an online Kundalini class was offered by the treatment centre, and I signed up for that. Kundalini yoga is often referred to as the "awareness yoga". Awareness was certainly something I had been learning and exploring, and I wanted to learn more as I found it enlightening. I found that if I started my day this way, it created some calm and set my day up for success. After each meditation or yoga practice, I would journal my thoughts, challenges, and successes in terms of recovery.

Daily Journaling: I hoped journaling would also provide me with aha moments or realizations about my past that would turn into lessons learned. I had started a journal at treatment and utilized this method for several months by this point, so I wanted to continue the practice.

The plan was pretty simple and was not near as comprehensive as the treatment centre had suggested, but I wanted to ensure success, so baby steps were my approach. I know that it is deep in my nature to be easily overwhelmed, so I chose to start with a plan that was doable and successful for me. I knew that at any time I could add to the plan, and for sure, I would revisit it in six months and revise it.

Regarding the Twelve Steps, I had worked through the first five steps at treatment, but I hadn't done anything more on that front. Some worked the steps with their sponsor, others worked the steps with a small group, but the steps at this point were not on my six-month plan. I was completely aware that the plan might need to change, but for now I decided to follow "my way".

Some would say that that was a risky move, and I knew that I needed to keep relapse signs at the top of my mind. One of the courses I took at Cedars was about the Warning Signs of Relapse, and to this day, I periodically review this document to keep myself in check. Letting go of an established routine was a big sign of relapse, so I knew that following my plan throughout would be critical. Plans have to be flexible too. Take away an aspect, add an aspect. The key for me was to consider the warning signs every day, and if I started to lose focus, I knew I had to get back on track. I keep my sobriety top of mind every day, and ask the truth of myself: "Am I being true to myself?" Nearly four years in, this is still my top priority.

Aside from the plan, I was of course back home and back into daily life. At first, I stayed close to home. I knew deep down that I was nervous about seeing people and particularly about them asking questions as to where I had been, and how I would answer them.

I knew that there were a few choices on that front. I could a.) Tell them I was at rehab and explain in full; b.) Tell them I was away looking after some health issues with no further explanation; or c.) Totally lie and say that I was around, and I guess we just hadn't crossed paths. We had "practised" our responses during the last week at the treatment centre. The boldest answer I heard from someone who had attended the facility twice was: "I am a proud alcoholic in recovery, and I was attending treatment." Period. I knew I wasn't ready for that explanation, but I finally decided to take it as it comes and reply in my comfort zone at the time.

I think that sometimes we as humans insist on overwhelming ourselves with worry. Worry serves no purpose, and I knew that, but it sure is hard to follow that reasoning. There was a gathering of a few of Roger's friends at one point, and no one said anything. So, regardless of where my thoughts went, the bottom line is that these people didn't even know I was away. Was that a good thing? A bad thing? Another time, I was asked by an acquaintance about not being around lately, and I simply said I was visiting on the Island.

As time went on, I wanted to share my journey with people close to me, but I didn't feel it was necessary to put out an announcement to the city that I had been in a treatment centre. A couple of closer friends were aware, and welcomed me back with congratulations for taking the first steps.

Then there were some friends that we were having sushi with at one of their homes. We were offered drinks, which Roger and I declined, and we were asked why we were not partaking as it had been our norm. I remembered hesitating, and then I looked over to Roger for his thoughts. Seeing his nod of approval, I said, "Let's take the elephant out of the room," and I proceeded to tell them about where I had been all summer. It was interesting that they had plenty of questions, and the conversation also included mention of some of their relatives who perhaps would benefit from such an "adventure".

We did talk about being ready for rehab. It is my believe that forcing someone to rehab would not work. You have to be ready for yourself and totally committed to the process and the new outcome. Going to treatment to satisfy parents, spouses, siblings, etc. does not work unless you are committed to the process.

I met people at rehab who were obviously just going through the paces as they had been sent there, or they had had an intervention and felt they had no choice. In my mind, an intervention could work, but only if the participant was committed to do the work. I met a couple of people sent there by a judge; the alternative being jail. One chap in particular was just biding his time to leave and resume his life of dealing drugs. He was quite upfront with other participants on this issue, and I assume the administration got wind of his comments, as he quietly disappeared a short time later. Another young lady I met was sent by her parents, who in her mind, were dead wrong about her addiction. She was there to have some time away from them and their "nagging", as she put it. How do you think that worked out?

THE FIFTH STAIR: NEW LESSONS

I would not want to imply that the journey is easy. IT IS NOT!

—Me!

*Recovery is not a google map—
you keep driving and sometimes hit a dead end…*

—Author Unknown

About a month after coming home, my routine was settling into place, and I was happy with that. It was Day 74, according to my journal. I did my meditation in the morning, and then we went for a wonderful walk on a crisp October day. The river valley in our city is beautiful, and the leaves of the trees were in full fall mode. I had been reading Eckhart Tolle's *The Power of Now* and was recalling the section of the book that suggested that we often spent time worrying about the future or regretting the past, instead of living each moment as it occurs. As I was walking, I was practising staying present. I was in awe of the nature around me and the feel of my feet crunching on the pathways.

When I returned home that day, for the first time, I felt that I wanted a drink. I had no idea why. Was it that I was feeling so good that I was thinking that I was "cured"? Was it the fact that I was happier now and that perhaps now all would be okay? I knew from my recovery plan, that this is a common thought during recovery, and it is also a trick. That's the thing with addiction. Your body has had a rest, and now your mind says, "Let's get back to 'life' as you knew it."

I recalled a conversation at the treatment centre when a crack cocaine addict said he was there to kick *that* habit and get back to smoking weed only. WRONG! We learned over and over that weed is perhaps not as potent, but it is still a mood-altering drug, legal or not, so we shouldn't be fooled that it is a potential solution. As time goes on, a person will increase their weed habit until it is simply not enough, particularly during challenging times. When that happens, it can become very tempting to slip back.

Similarly, I recall a lecture leader talking about their own battle thinking that he could replace the painkillers from sport injuries with a drink or two. He described that accelerating and, before he knew it, he was on the same path, just with a different poison.

This is according to the experts; it not just my opinion. The thought did cross my mind that perhaps I was ready to have only one drink and perhaps I could purchase some wine. That was my addiction talking, and talk it would many more times. When I would tell myself that perhaps I could try one glass, I recalled learning that was my EGO talking, and it would always think it knew best. But my clear mind said otherwise. The feeling was disturbing and made me feel anxious. I talked about it on one of the recovery meetings, and I found that talking with like-minded people really helped.

The following day, the same feelings came over me. I really didn't understand what the trigger was, or why now. However, I once again talked to someone about it, and the feeling moved through me.

That evening, while in a recovery meeting, the counsellor made a statement, which took me back, given my thoughts the last couple of days. He said: " If something feels off, pay attention to that." In addiction and early recovery, we as alcoholics or addicts are very selfish. We plan our time around our drug of choice schedule and lose our awareness of others around us. It was certainly a goal of mine to get back to living my definition of success, which included listening to others and to my internal intuition. I took a tool from the toolkit I had from Cedars and put it front and centre:

S.T.O.P.
S = Stop (do nothing)
T = Take a breath (or breathe until you are more relaxed)
O = Observe (What are you feeling?)
P = Proceed (when you feel calm again. Now you can respond if you need to).

Or another technique that I find useful is:

H.A.L.T.
Am I **H**ungry? Am I **A**ngry? Am I **L**onely? Am I **T**ired?

This is a quick check-point when you are feeling anxious. When I utilize it, I am reminded about focus, and work my way through the moment. I remembered that I had learned that your addiction wants to keep you sick. Your physical body wants the old pleasure to return. It is at these times, in particular, when you need to take the time to ground yourself and reach out to talk about it. Talk to a friend who understands your journey, talk to a counsellor, talk to a sponsor, or talk about it at a recovery meeting. You can even call the treatment centre and talk to the staff in the intake department, who are experts. This is a good practice for me. I had daily meetings at my fingertips and also the phone numbers of dozens of people with whom I had gone to recovery. You can reach out to other friends and relatives, but bear in mind they may not be as intimately acquainted with recovery. Sometimes, I would just pick up my journal and write it out, and then discuss it at my next meeting.

There is a book that we used daily at rehab called *Just for Today— Daily Meditations for Recovering Addicts*. It is produced by the NA community. Although I was given this book in the treatment centre, you can purchase this book from a variety of outlets online. At rehab, we had a daily meeting at which we read the page for the day. We then talked in a small group about how it applied to our current thoughts, what we had learned from the "lesson", and/or how we could apply it today.

I found this simple book motivational, for the most part. Somewhere around Day 90, I was invited to a Zoom women's meeting to continue the "Just for Today practice". I was participating at one of my recovery meetings online, and one of the leaders of the woman's meeting put some information about their group in the chat room. I found great value in a smaller intimate group, as I had at the treatment centre, so I was anxious to join up.

At the first meeting, I met a number of women, some of whom were affected by alcohol and some by drugs. I had not met any of them in person at the treatment centre as they were all about six months to a year ahead of me. We met weekly first thing in the morning, and this quickly became another staple in my practice. I enjoyed the other participants and learning about their journeys, which were ahead of mine. That was an advantage for me, as it didn't seem to matter what challenge I was facing or what question I had, as someone in this small group could speak with experience to the issue.

An example of a JFT lesson was on August 27: "Just for today, I will choose life by choosing recovery. I will take care of myself." The reading goes on for no more than one page, so it is a simple addition to your new routine. As time went on, I too invited others to join our small group. Our group met for well over a year, and although I never met most of the participants in person, the discussions in general were helpful and supportive. The group fell off a bit as participants were starting to return to work or look for work. For myself, I was retired, so I didn't have to face that challenge.

I was regularly attending the Kundalini yoga classes offered through the rehab centre and enjoying them, particularly the meditation parts. I was starting to understand the spiritual side of the practice. At first it is hard to stay focused on meditation if you are not used to it. You hear a sound, and your mind wanders. However, as time went on, I found that I was starting to be much more focused during the meditation. When I first started the practice, it was hard to turn off the "monkey brain". You know, making a to-do list while "meditating", thinking about something that happened yesterday, or something that is happening next week. Be persistent, and it does get easier, and it is worth the wait!

Progress Not Perfection

At the six-month mark, I was starting to notice some real tangible changes in my outlook, attitude, and reactions to events and people.

As an example, I had an ornery neighbour, who I will call Grumpy Joe. For years, he created dissension between neighbours. He approached contractors and visitors as if they were coming over enemy lines by driving into our bungalow complex. His language, his shouting, and waving of his finger was almost famous around the area. I have, as many have, had disagreements and arguments with him on numerous occasions. Just to see him drive by made my blood boil.

One day I realized that when I saw him, my reaction was no longer anger, but rather I thought: *What an angry and lonely existence Grumpy Joe must have.* I wondered what had happened in his life of seventy-five-plus years that made him the way he is. *Perhaps he isn't even aware of his demeanour, and isn't that sad?* Big change in my thought process!

Around Christmas, I decided to make tourtières as gifts for friends. If you aren't familiar, a tourtière is a French-Canadian meat pie. It has been a family tradition of mine to make it for either Christmas Eve or New Year's Day dinner. It is very time consuming to make pies for eight different people/families. Over the years, I knew that many a time I felt angry at "all I do for others, without any thanks." I remembered sending gifts to siblings and a couple of friends, and at times never hearing back—no thank you, no acknowledgement whatsoever. It made me furious, and I would vow to cut them from the "list".

I also sent out about eighty Christmas cards every year, often with a short letter, and would receive less than half back. Again, I would vow to remove people off the list, justifying it as they were unappreciative and probably didn't care anyway. I never really cut down the list, but the same feelings would emerge the following year, and once again, I would vow to cut back the "giving".

This first Christmas season of recovery, I starting pulling together Christmas plans and making lists. I was happily baking the pies, and reminiscing about learning to make pastry with my mom, who had passed earlier in the year. The lightbulb lit up, and I realized that I was not doing this as a chore or because I had to anymore. I was making these gifts for people I cared about.

Similarly, I wrote out the eighty or so Christmas cards. My expectations of a return gift or card were gone. I genuinely wanted to reach out and wish the best of the season to those I cared about. Wow, I was doing these things for the right reasons, which hadn't been the case for a very long time.

Later that evening, I was on a AA Zoom meeting, and we were talking about giving back to those we cared for. Someone on the call said that for him, "Recovery was his gift" to himself and his loved ones that Christmas. Another participant said, "I get up on time out of respect for myself, and that is my gift." Both of these comments really stuck with me. Gifts are not only physical items; they are also gestures and kind words. They are also reaching out just to chat, say thank you for being my friend, or expressing your love and caring. I knew this in my head, but was starting to see that I was knowing this in my heart as well.

I wanted that momentum to continue, so I consciously added being less judgemental to my goals of recovery. I wanted to catch myself when I became judgemental and ultimately be naturally nonjudgemental without a second thought. A part of my definition of success was to "make a difference". Generally, I believe I am a kind human, but I knew at times my demeanour was sometimes out of societal expectations. I wanted kindness to my fellow human to not be out of obligation, but out of being totally genuine.

By the end of six months, I had had many days without sleep, or at least very little sleep. I would awaken frustrated that I was not "cured" and found that the lack of sleep was coming out as irritability and frustration. I had to remind myself that I would never be "cured". My recovery is my new journey, and that journey was for the rest of my days. I continued re-reading my journals, searching for lessons learned, and I knew that as time went on, it would get better and better. I knew from my studies that my body and mind were still adjusting and that I needed to persevere and trust the process. I remember learning at treatment that your physical body would take some time to get used to "coping without aids". My meetings, my journaling, my Kundalini, and my meditations were my staples, and for that I was grateful.

A colleague in the Just for Today group introduced us to a new version of the "Serenity Prayer" meant more for women and how hard we are on ourselves.

The Other Serenity Prayer

*Goddess, grant me the serenity to stop beating
myself up for not doing things perfectly,
The courage to forgive myself because I am
working on being better,
And the wisdom to know that you already
love me just the way I am.*

—Author Unknown

The last six months of Year One were also challenging. I was committed to my plan and adding to it in small bits, and it was working for me. One afternoon in March (after about eight months of sobriety), I was listening to an interesting podcast by Eckhart Tolle called *The Path to Inner Peace*. He talked about giving your full attention to the "little bits". For example, being mindful to the feel of the crisp fall air and to the steps you are taking as you walk around the neighbourhood, as well as paying attention to your interactions with others, focusing on making eye contact, and really seeing those around you.

It was interesting, and I thought it would be a new area to study and learn about moving forward.

Later in the day, we got a call from my husband's surgeon: Roger had cancer.

Recovery is messy, just like life is messy

Watching for events, people, places, and things that potentially could send me spiralling back into addiction was a key part of my journey. I thought perhaps this could be one of those times, but in truth, it was the opposite: the news actually gave me strength. Concern and love for my life partner and the journey that was about to start for us amplified my courage. I needed to be the strong one to help him through this. I needed to bring the positivity and encouragement, just as Roger had done for me nine months ago. The diagnosis was difficult to hear, but the optimism of the doctors was encouraging. It started with a difficult, lengthy surgery shortly after the news. The cancer centre and their staff in our city is amazing. Roger started on an immune therapy treatment, which would go on for about a year, along with physiotherapy and speech therapy. Today, over nearly four later, his health continues to be excellent.

In a group therapy meeting on the evening we had heard the original news, someone on the call said that in tough times you need to live the solution, not the problem, and to stop with any futurizing about potential outcomes. I remember a counsellor at the treatment centre saying that addicts/alcoholics are notorious for making mountains out of molehills.

Roger and I had many conversations about one day (or step) at a time. This is a common phrase in the recovery world, but it took on new meaning with this new journey we were embarking on. We decided to not get ahead of ourselves and focus only on the next treatment, the next CT scan, the next appointment, etc., and not any further ahead. It worked beautifully. We also wanted to only be around positive energy and not the "woe-is-me" crowd. We made that clear to those around us and it worked.

It is interesting that you see "helpers" along the way when you need them. The day of the announcement about the upcoming cancer treatment plan, my Just for Today reading said: "True courage is not the absence of fear, but rather the willingness to walk through it." Sometimes you just can't ignore what the universe is telling you.

The Sixth Stair: Exploring Options

*There is no one fail-safe way out of addiction.
Nothing works for everyone.
We need to find the right path for ourselves.
Twelve steps, five steps, no steps, eight steps:
what is right is what works.*

—Gabor Maté, MD

Gabor Maté is a Canadian physician who has shared his expertise on many topics including addiction, stress, and childhood trauma. His latest book is called the *Myth of Normal*. He is well known in the addiction world and resides in Vancouver. He also practises Kundalini yoga.

I was introduced to the Twelve Steps and Traditions of Alcoholics Anonymous during treatment. I list them here in case you are not familiar. I was not familiar with them before attending treatment.

The Twelve Steps

1. We admitted we were powerless over alcohol—that our lives had become unmanageable.

2. Came to believe that a Power greater than ourselves could restore us to sanity.

3. Made a decision to turn our will and our lives over to the care of God as we understood Him.

4. Made a searching and fearless moral inventory of ourselves.

5. Admitted to God, to ourselves, and to another human being the exact nature of our wrongs.

6. Were entirely ready to have God remove all of these defects of character.

7. Humbly asked Him to remove our shortcomings.

8. Made a list of all persons we had harmed, and became willing to make amends to them all.

9. Made direct amends to such people wherever possible, except when to do so would injure them or others.

10. Continued to take personal inventory, and when we were wrong, promptly admitted it.

11. Sought through prayer and meditation to improve our conscious contact with God as we understood Him, praying only for knowledge of His will for us and the power to carry that out.

12. Having had a spiritual awakening as the result of these steps, we tried to carry this message to alcoholics, and to practise these principles in all our affairs.

Note: "God" refers to your power greater than yourself. It could be another spiritual force such as Buddha, Allah, Nature, Creator, etc.

Those steps and traditions were written by men for men in and around 1939. At that time, women generally were in the workforce primarily to assist with the war effort. However, soon after that, women were replaced by men, whose role was to be the primary breadwinner. Women were then expected to resume their role as homemakers and supporters of their men. Women were still promising to "obey" in their marriage vows around that time, and if they did work, it was generally for lower wages.

The original AA books were not geared towards the "fairer" sex and were revised many times over the years. Even with that, many women I have met over the last few years are drawn to another book also endorsed by AA: *A Woman's Way Through the Twelve Steps* written by Stephanie S. Covington, Ph.D.

The female voice is more relatable for many women I know. The examples and stories in these alternate books are more modern, and easier to absorb and apply. This was particularly true for several women I met who turned to alcohol in part because of abusive relationships they had been/were in. I remember meeting "Jane" who shared with me that there was no way any man's words were going to change her mind about what she needed to work on, let alone how she was going to work on sobriety! The book also comes with a workbook, which is handy if the reader is working on the Twelve Steps.

I suggest this set of books if AA/NA resonates with you, and you are planning to work the steps either in a small women's group or with your sponsor.

Remembering that we are not all Christians in this world, another interesting book that I read during my first year of sobriety was from Buddha's teachings. I have always been fascinated by Buddha's teachings, as I find them more relatable and easier to understand than many traditional Christian books. This text was written by Valerie Mason-John and Dr. Paramabandhu Groves. It is called *Eight Step Recovery: Using the Buddha's Teachings to Overcome Addiction*. Here are the eight steps:

The Eight Steps Toward Recovery:

1. Accepting that this human life will bring suffering
2. Seeing how we create extra suffering in our lives
3. Embracing impermanence to show us that our suffering can end
4. Being willing to step onto the path of recovery and discover freedom
5. Transforming our speech, actions, and livelihood
6. Placing positive values at the centre of our lives
7. Making every effort to stay on the path of recovery
8. Helping others by sharing the benefits we have gained

I also have a number of acquaintances that find another Buddhist approach, often called "Refuge Recovery", to be an easier, systematic approach to recovery. There was some controversy over the founder of Refuge at some point, but the principles are still useful.

The Four Truths

1. Addiction creates suffering
2. The cause of addiction is repetitive craving
3. Recovery is possible
4. The path to recovery is available

Another recovery "system" to explore is SMART Recovery. The acronym stands for Self-Management and Recovery Training. At the treatment centre I was at, a small group that had been to treatment before were participating in SMART. The goal of SMART Recovery is to help a person in treatment overcome the type of self-defeating thinking that hinders long-term sobriety and leads to relapse.

The Four SMART Principles

1. Building and maintaining motivation
2. Coping with urges
3. Managing thoughts, feelings, and behaviours
4. Living a balanced life

SMART Recovery does not use a step-by-step process as AA/NA does, but rather is based on continual growth and learning from experiences building on an individual's strengths.

Somewhere in my journey I learned of the Four Indigenous Spiritual Laws, which impacted me and my way of thinking. The Four North American Spirituality Laws say that nothing happens without a reason in life. When you truly understand this, it becomes easier to handle what is happening in your life.

The Four North American Spirituality Laws

Law #1: *The person you meet is the right one.*

That is, no one comes into our lives by accident. All the people around us are there for a reason, either to educate us or to help us in our current situation in life.

Law #2: *What happens is the only thing that can happen.*

Nothing, absolutely nothing, that happens to us could have been different. There is no, "If I had done it differently, it would have been different…" No, what happened was the only way it could happen, so that we can learn the lesson to move on. Everything—yes, every situation that happens to us in life—is absolutely perfect, even when our spirit resists our ego and doesn't want to accept it.

Law #3: *Every moment when something starts is the right time.*

Every moment comes at the right time, not sooner or later. When we are ready for something new in our life, it is already there to begin.

Law #4: *What is over, is over.*

It is that simple. When something ends in our lives, it serves us to learn from it and move on, based on the experiences we have gained.

Just before I finished this book, I found dozens of helpful groups on Instagram including *She Walks Canada*. Many of these groups offer events, meetings and coaching for those in recovery. All methods of getting and staying clean/sober have merit. The self-help section of your local bookstore will offer dozens of options around recovery, preventing relapse, staying clean and sober, etc.

I personally spent a lot of time researching and attending meetings of various methods. The absolute key for me was finding the bits that resonated with me. Then I incorporated them into my recovery plan and committed 100% to following that plan.

In addition, another commitment to myself was to revisit "the plan" at least twice a year, and revise it as needed.

The Seventh Stair: Expanding My Understanding

Just as trees shed their leaves in winter and renew themselves, the mind can shed its prejudices, barriers, and renew itself.

—Radha Burnier, Indian Film Actress and 5 terms as President of the Theosophical Society

would like to tell a story from my days in rehabilitation that to this day makes me stop and listen to all around me. I met "Sam", an Indigenous man, about halfway through my treatment. Outside of the meal hall, there was a peaceful pond that was home to a few koi fish. I loved sitting there, listening to the water as I gathered my thoughts, and often could be found there journaling or working on my homework. One day after lunch, Sam asked if he could join me, and we introduced ourselves. He was only about forty years old he told me, but he looked much older. He even said to me, "You probably thought I was older. I have had a tough life."

He went on to tell me that he was raised by several older siblings. As I recall, he was the youngest of seven children. He said that he had no recollection of his father, and never knew what happened to him. His older siblings had told him that their father had left, and that was all he knew. He vaguely remembered his mother, but said she passed away many years ago as a result of alcohol addiction. He suspected it was more than alcohol, but wasn't sure. At some point as a teen, he left "home" and had been, for the most part, living on the streets of a small town in the province.

That day, Sam and I discussed what had brought each of us to the treatment centre. I explained that I no longer wanted to live my life the way I had been. I knew for sure that I didn't want to continue destroying my life and my health, and I wanted to work on protecting my relationships in my life that were meaningful to me. Sam nodded, and we sat in silence for a few minutes.

I broke the silence and asked how he had gotten to this place we found ourselves in. He hesitated, and then said that he had asked his Chief to be sent to this facility. He knew of others from his band who had come here in hopes of full recovery, and he had seen some of them succeed. But then he continued and said that recovery was not possible for him and that he asked to come for other reasons.

He went on to tell me that he was dying due to a liver disease. The doctors had said that his time was near. He said that he could not recall a time in his entire life that alcohol was not a daily part of his time on this earth. He remembered drinking when his age was still in the single digits. Then he looked me straight in the eye, and said, "I asked to come here, so that I could live a brief time without clouded eyes."

He went on about how beautiful the land was around us, how good the food and the bed provided were, and also how wonderful the helpers (staff) were. Here was a dying man expressing his gratitude for all that surrounded him. I can picture this conversation, and exactly where we were sitting as if it were yesterday. We sat together the following day as well, and continued our discussion. Then after that, I never saw him again. I do think of Sam often and his bravery to ask his Chief for the opportunity that was given to him in his final days. Remembering his words, I give thanks for all that I have in this world.

I am embarrassed to say that, as a Canadian who was brought up in a mostly white, privileged world, I had been living in some sort of bubble. I knew no one who had lived lives like many people of the people I encountered at the centre, including Sam.

I believe that conversation is the start of understanding, so I set a new goal in my recovery. I wanted to gain some education about the Indigenous people who were in these territories long before my ancestors crossed the ocean. I was vaguely aware of some of the injustices, but I wanted to understand and learn more.

The first book I was pointed towards was a book that in part takes place in my home city of Edmonton: *In My Own Moccasins: A Memoir of Resilience* by Helen Knott, who was named a RBC Taylor Prize Emerging Writer in 2020. This is an outstanding memoir that she wrote first and foremost for her people. She is very clear about this point and why she wrote this piece.

There is a passage in the introduction of the book that spoke to me. Ms. Knott talks about it being suggested to her that her book could be an excellent tool to teach others about the impact of violence, racism and colonialism in many Indigenous women's lives.

She makes it clear that if we as 'others' learn from the book, that would be a good outcome, even though she wrote it for herself and her people.

I agree with Ms. Knott that things will not change in the world without all humans/races/genders attempting to understand each other. At the very least we should all be attempting to be more open to listening to other viewpoints. I believe that the more we can learn of others, the more we can understand, and with that, we can better communicate and appreciate each other for our differences.

This section of the book was powerful. I knew that I wanted to bury my judgements and join the conversation moving forward.

The second book that was suggested to me was *Life in the City of Dirty Water: A Memoir of Healing* by Clayton Thomas-Muller. Mr. Thomas-Muller is a member of the Cree Nation Pukatawagan in Northern Manitoba. Not only does Mr. Thomas-Muller talk of his upbringing, domestic and sexual abuse, and the residential school system in Canada, but also his commitment to addressing environmental injustices on Indigenous lands by the oil industry. This book was a real eye-opener for me in more ways than one.

I also went to the Aboriginal People's Television Network (APTN) and took a three-part course on the history of Residential Schools in Canada. It was called First Contact. I was so ill-informed as to the extent of the injustices that went on in this aspect of our nation's history. Reading these books and taking this course was just a tiny drop in the bucket, I know, but if we all took the time to understand some of the root causes of some of society's woes, perhaps we could be better as humans on this planet.

At the time of this writing, I continue to seek out and expand my knowledge and understanding of people that come from a culture religion different to mine.

The Eighth Stair: Celebrate!

Every morning before leaving my bed I say thank you. I don't want to walk into the sunset anymore, I want to run into the sunrise. I am filled to the brim with gratitude.

—Jann Arden, Singer, Songwriter, Author

When I read Jann's Arden's book *If I Knew Then: Finding Wisdom in Failure and Power in Aging*, I related to her struggles and loved the above quotation. What I knew for sure, to borrow a phrase from Oprah, was that I was no longer in the dark shadows of myself, and I was determined not to ever be there again. Also, to borrow a saying from Meghan, my Kundalini leader: "Run towards your shadows, and you will be set free. The more you let go, the more you can invite in."

The first time I was in the dark shadows of myself was many years ago around my fortieth birthday. I decided to end my life around that time, a time when my daughters were away on vacation with their dad and his new wife. I spent time in the psychiatric ward of the hospital, followed by daily therapy for many months. It took a lot of therapy, and tremendous support from friends, in particular my friend Joanne, before I was able to start climbing out of that depression. I described it as falling into the "black hole"; the sides of that hole were muddy and slippery. Yes, I got out of that hole, and I recall thinking: *That's that, don't want to go there again!* Then I continued my life. It is apparent now that there hadn't been enough therapy to change the course of the next twenty years or so, but there was a good stretch of happiness.

I know that I have to continue my recovery journey for the rest of my days. As Jann says, "I want to run into the sunrise." I was in a beautiful place of gratitude for my life and my sobriety. My spirit was rising, not falling.

July 20th: One Year Sobriety. Excerpt from my Journal: *I had an amazing Just for Today group meeting. My friend, Leonie made it so special. She came to the meeting (Zoom) with a one-year coin, a candle, and read out a touching poem she wrote for me. Roger brought me two dozen yellow roses and tickets to the van Gogh art show, which I really wanted to attend. I was able to bask in the amazing interactive show around me, loving the serenity of peacefulness and joy and alone time with my thoughts and senses. My appreciation for this amazing artist, who himself led a tortured life, was over the top.*

Taking time by yourself, with no other agenda than just being mindful of your surroundings is so calming. Taking a walk and noting the trees, flowers, snow, rain, people ... with no judgement. Sitting in a favourite chair, listening to the words of music, or listening to the piano keys soothes your soul. Watching the birds as they go about their nest building, and most of all, being fully awake in our lives.

Over the course of a week or so, with my journal in hand, I started to formulate my second year. I knew if I just went about everyday life, that my present state of mind could slip away so easily. As hard as I was working on my sobriety, I was still fragile, and I knew that. I was beginning to realize that not having sobriety, peace, calm, and mindfulness top of mind could lead me down the slippery slope.

So let the planning begin!

Listen to Your Soul

Here are some of my journal notes that helped me nail down the second-year plan. This was a sort of self-brainstorming. I took out some blank paper and my pencil crayons and drew "bubbles" that I put each activity in:

What does the next year look like? Sobriety is a given. Reading more about other people's journey's and taking lessons from their words. The journeys need not be recovery related.

I plan to read more about people's journeys of courage, perseverance, and resilience, in particular women.

I so enjoyed the van Gogh exhibition, that more "arts" in my life is part of the plan—the art gallery, the new museum in my city, participating in festivals, more artistic expression from myself, perhaps sewing or making quilts for those I love and care about. I plan to get out in nature more, appreciating all that nature can teach me about life—perhaps going to the raspberry farm and picking fruit, walking in the river valley.

I want to focus on "living" my definition of success that I wrote back in the 1990s. I want to be more tolerant of others. You don't know what others have experienced in life, or what struggles and triumphs they have had. All of our life experiences shape who we are as people. I know this in my head, but I want to apply it from my heart.

That is not to say that I will tolerate or engage those who are spewing negativity around me. Depending on my relationship with the person, I will take different approaches: ignore it, walk away, express my opinion, but I will not engage in it. In other words, if there are inappropriate comments, let's say about race or sexuality, I am not going to engage in the laughter or the joke or the mockery that others may find amusing. In some cases, I will express my opinion in no uncertain terms.

My experience with those that engage in these types of comments are, in my opinion, generally naive or un-educated in cultures or practices that are different to theirs. As I have said in the past, listening goes a long way to try to understand the differences. Education of cultures different from your own also goes a long way to understanding. I have a sense that broadening my knowledge will contribute to more happiness and joy in my life.

Year two will be a year to focus more on moving away from negative energy. I find that more and more, when the conversation becomes negative, woe is me, or similar, I walk away. I know of many people who see the world from the gloomy side first, or the glass is half empty to phrase it another way. I want more connection with people, but likeminded people. People who see the positive before the negative; people who accept others and their cultures, rather than judging them.

I truly want to live one experience at a time, one day at a time. This not only applied to remaining clean and sober, but also to my life with

Roger. His treatments are going very well, and we are optimistic.

I will also continue my group therapy, and my Kundalini practice with the treatment centre.

Around this time of formulating my plan, I met a woman at a farmer's market. She was selling a book she wrote. For some reason, I was drawn to her, so I stood from a distance watching her interact with people. From a distance, she appeared very quiet and reserved, and perhaps a bit uncomfortable with selling her book. A man, presumably her partner, sat beside her. Also, I felt like I knew her, but couldn't place her. It was something about her demeanour that re-enforced this feeling.

Then I noticed the cover of her book; it was colourful, with a picture of feathers, and it appeared to be a little girl walking into the light. On top of that, the title of the book was about making amends. One of the steps of AA is making amends to those who you have hurt during your using days. Perhaps it was a bit bold, but I asked if she was in recovery and if it was a true story. She said it was fiction, but it certainly had true elements. I felt instantly connected to her and her spirit. I bought two copies and sent one to a friend in recovery.

The connection I felt with this human being was powerful, and I wasn't sure how to explain it, but for weeks afterwards, my mind was still trying to figure out how I "knew" her, even though we had not met.

I believe that everything happens for a reason; every person who comes into your life is there for a reason. The challenge is recognizing this and not questioning why someone crosses your path, but rather just trusting the process.

After reading the book, I knew that adding spirituality to my second-year list was a given. Perhaps that was the reason I met the author, as her book was filled with spirituality, and it inspired me. But in what form that would take, I had no idea yet. My friend Leonie sent me this quote which I love:

> *"TIME decides who you meet in your life.*
> *HEART decides who you want in your life.*
> *BEHAVIOUR decides who will stay in your life."*

—Ziad Abdelmour, Lebanese-American Author

Goal Setting

My second year was starting out strong with my goals for the year set out. Loosely set out, that is. I had always been very structured in my life, and I felt that perhaps that could use some shake up. My days were always so structured, and that left little room for reflection and/or solitude, and I wanted more of that mindful behaviour in my life.

I decided to continue with group therapy as I still found great wisdom and food for thought in those meetings. I found the sessions very helpful when I was struggling as well. The facilitator always called out the truth, and that was a continued need of mine. No more sugar coating, please! I don't think there was a session that went by that I didn't have a valuable take-away.

I also decided for this second year to drop, for the time being anyway, the recovery meetings that were chaired by fellow alcoholics and addicts. These meetings were sponsored by the treatment centre. Much of the content of late was centred around having a sponsor and working the steps in a systematic way, but that was not working for me. I knew I could come back to it, but for now, no. I carry with me the Zoom code and password in my phone just in case I feel the need.

My twice-a-week Kundalini class was still wonderful. The breathing, calm, and spiritual meditations were powerful. My teacher was developing her website further, and I was able to invest in some of her new classes and meditations on my own on the alternate days to her live teachings. Therefore, a daily meditation or class was a new part of my routine. For me, they put me in the right frame of mind for the day, along with my journaling.

A note on journaling: One of the powerful parts of my journaling was looking back in time and seeing the progression of my thoughts. For me to read a notation from a year prior and realize that my reactions had changed in some cases was worth the effort of the writing. It also re-enforced areas that still needed some work! I am, just as you reading this are, human. As humans, we can be creatures of habit, and changing some of those habits takes time and hard work. Seeing baby steps come to fruition is gratifying, and it encourages me to continue the journey.

As time went on, I realized that something was stirring deep in my belly. I felt energized and excited about the journey. The first year was tough in terms of adjusting, healing, and finding love for myself and JOY.

Here is an excerpt from my journal in that second year:

August 8, 2022: *Last evening, we went out with friends for dinner. It was a lot of fun. I missed being social with others. Some had alcoholic drinks, but it didn't faze me ... no thoughts of wishing I could have one, no flashbacks, no cravings. I thought to myself,* You're getting there, Cheryl. *My JFT reading that particular day was about not looking back and not regretting the past, but rather learning from it. I was looking at living a calmer life, and I still had a long way to go, but I was willing and ready!*

I realize today that I am not harbouring as many resentments towards certain people around me. One by one, I am focusing on these past hurts, shames, and resentments and letting them go. Some of the teachings from my Kundalini classes are assisting with that. I also know that my tolerance of others that are obviously struggling is quite different. I saw a homeless person today, and I felt for them; specifically, I could recognize their pain and struggle. I hope that one day they will have the blessed opportunity that I had in terms of healing. In the meantime, I am happy to help them out with a bit of change or something to eat. I see many homeless hanging around the farmer's market I go to in Strathcona and have engaged in many a conversation with some of the regulars.

Earlier in my recovery, I was given a book called *Everyday Mindfulness—365 Days to a Centred Life* by Abby Willowroot. At the time, I decided to read the thought for the day when I got up and try to live it throughout that day. Here is an example of one of the day's thoughts:

Make me strong in spirit, courageous in action, gentle of heart, let me act in wisdom, conquer my fear and doubt, discover my own hidden gifts, meet others with compassion, be a source of healing energies, and face each day with hope and joy.

That reading says it all to me. There are many days that I feel my heart and soul expanding. That may not make sense at first, but let me try to explain. When I am in a place of true mindfulness, I look around me and truly feel appreciation for my senses: seeing, hearing, feeling, sensing, communicating. For example, I am looking out of my writing room at my small tree outside. Yesterday I could see up close that the buds were present and about to burst. The buds were just waiting for the universe to say it was the right time. Then, last evening, after a few weeks of hot and dry weather, the rain came. I heard it in my dreams. I felt the damp as I cozied under my quilts, which I made with love. Now this morning, I gaze out to my tiny garden, and the leaves have been "born". They are beautiful, and soon they will burst with lilacs. Nature at work.

About a month after this experience, we noticed that a pair of robins were building a nest in that same tree, and we watched daily in fascination. One of the pair, let's say it was papa, was keeping watch on the roof of the house next door, while the mama was returning with chunks of dry grass and a bit of mud. She would land on the wrought iron post near the tree, chirp to her partner, who it appeared was giving the "all-clear", and then would dive into the tree to place the latest piece of material for the nest. At the time of this writing, the eggs have hatched, and we are watching mama and papa bringing a plethora of worms to the new ones. We are awaiting flight school to start soon.

Around the two-year mark, I went searching for the "perfect" reflection-reading chair. It took a while, but when I saw it; I knew she was the one! I love this chair, with a felt bag of books beside it. On the table sits numerous pairs of reading specs, in a variety of colours. (The brand Peepers are a favourite.) Okay, I will admit, there are probably at least twelve pairs. Aside from reading into the early evening instead of watching television, I can often be found sitting in my special chair, closing my eyes, and truly listening to the poetry of a song. I try to listen to each of the notes, envision my fingers on a piano keyboard, and truly hear each of the words. Try doing this listening to Leonard Cohen's "Hallelujah". Clear your mind and truly hear and feel the words of this great poet.

Sit, or stand right now, close your eyes, and listen.
   Yes, just listen.
      Really hear the sounds around you.
         Feel the goosebumps as you think of the miracles that have come your way.
           Can you hear a bird nearby?
              Can you hear voices in the background?
           Breathe deeply and listen.

Living mindfully is a part of my healing practice, and over the three years before starting this book, I saw that my mindfulness was growing constantly and bringing me more and more joy. It takes time and regular practice to live this way. I am sure I am a long way off from the experts, but I love this work in progress! More on Mindfulness in the next chapter.

The Ninth Stair: Mindfulness & Positivity

*Life is too short to argue and fight with the past.
Count your blessings, value your loved ones,
and move on with your head held high.*

—Author Unknown

was beginning to see that life is short. Of course, we have all heard that expression, but have you ever taken the time to think about it? Perhaps you have, BUT what did you do about it? What are you doing in your everyday life to make the most of today, and when tomorrow comes, how will you make the most of that day?

Earlier I mentioned the book called *Everyday Mindfulness—365 Days to a Centred Life*. Here is the definition of mindfulness at the start of the book:

> *Mindfulness (noun):*
>
> *A mental state achieved by focusing one's awareness on the present moment, while calmly acknowledging and accepting one's feelings, thoughts, and bodily sensations.*

I listened to a teaching podcast around this time by Eckhart Tolle. You may want to check out his website eckharttolle.com to learn about a variety of his teachings, and seminars. One of the profound statements I heard was the following:

> *Wherever you are, be there totally. If you find your here and now is intolerable, and it makes you unhappy, you have three options:*
>
> *Remove yourself from the situation;*
>
> *Change it; or*
>
> *Accept it totally ... Period!*

More and more, I was noticing the negativity around me: people complaining about their jobs, neighbours, and relatives. Even more noticeable was those who saw the negative first. You may recognize the one who, when asked how they are today, respond with: "Same sh__, another day." Or how about the person who responds with: "Okay, I guess, but…" These people are filled with yeah-buts, excuses, and blame for others; they do not take responsibility for their situation. If you don't like the way things are, change it, as Eckhart would say.

You can stay where you are in life and continue to complain about the same things over and over until the day you die. Or you can break free, stop complaining, and shift your focus to the positives. What would that look like? Easier said than done, but in my journey, I have learned that it is doable.

Take today, as you are reading this. Stop and commit to yourself to be positive for the rest of the day. Project yourself in a positive light, and look for the best in everyone you encounter today. Say "good morning", and mean it, without the expectation of an answer. Can you hear yourself, or someone else who says "good morning" in a droning, lacklustre way? Is that really a wish for good vibes for the day? No. They are using the words they were taught to greet another person. If you had responded with, "Not very well," they might have said, "That's good," as they walked away because they weren't really listening.

Practise this until it is second nature, and you don't have to think about it. Practise with the check-out person in the grocery store. Smile and ask how their day is or comment with positivity. In this way, you are inviting positivity into your own day/life. Wave to someone, talk to a stranger, just start somewhere … anywhere.

I remember a situation around this time, during which my husband was in the line-up at Tim Hortons, while I was waiting in the wings. There was an elderly gentleman sitting at a stool nearby, looking despondent. I greeted him with a cheery "good morning". He looked at me like I was crazy, but I continued by commenting about how wonderful it felt to have spring weather in the air.

He commented that, "There has been so much rain, and it is depressing."

I replied, "But, isn't that rain great? The farmers will be appreciative to have a good crop year."

He was still puzzled and replied, "Yah, I guess so."

So, I asked him, "What is the best thing about spring?"

He replied, "Well, I don't have to shovel snow!"

We both started to laugh. As I left, telling him to enjoy his day, he smiled broadly and said, "It was a pleasure talking to you."

Do you think I may have changed his day, just a little? I would like to think so. He felt better, and so did I as I walked away with a spring in my step. I heard an expression once, *"Leave footprints of kindness wherever you go."* I love that phrase. I am not sure where it came from, but wow, what a different world we would be living in if everyone followed that suggestion!

I could see that the calm, joy, and peace I was starting to discover was having a positive effect on me. I saw that love starts with me, and if I love myself, it is so much easier to navigate the world. Our current world certainly has its share of trouble these days, so a little kindness, perhaps, will help on that front. When I use positive language, gestures, and thoughts, and share that, it radiates from within, and people notice.

I was starting also to see that there is no use in blaming others for my woes. *How does blame help?* I asked myself. It certainly doesn't solve anything by complaining that someone else is at fault. Those negative energies need to be acknowledged and given away to the universe. I find it interesting when someone comments that their childhood was awful or their job is awful and then uses that as their primary reason (or excuse) for their behaviour. It may be that their childhood was indeed challenging, and the same with their job. However, think of it this way. There were probably awful events in that childhood or job, but it is unlikely that it all was terrible. In some cases, perhaps their childhood was indeed a nightmare, but they lived through it, and now they can live life differently. Now about the job, if it is so awful, start a plan to find another one for heaven's sake.

I was learning to focus on the positives. I was gradually finding ways to heal from negative events of the past, and then let them go. That does not mean that those events didn't happen, or that those events didn't hurt. Harbouring old grudges and events zaps your energy and will lead you to continue a sad, negative life. You only get one chance on the planet. Use it wisely, I now say.

I have learned that it is important to not repeat a pattern of negative experiences from the past. For example, let us say that you were abused by a family member as a child. That is major trauma, but what can you take from that? One lesson would be to ensure that the trend doesn't continue with your own children; you can become the first generation to not continue the thread. Perhaps you can learn to set firm boundaries with not only that person, but others in your life. Perhaps forgive yourself as it was not your fault. Perhaps take the positive lesson that now you know how to stand up for yourself and to speak out. I found that trying to find the positive in a negative situation is hard, but worth the exploration.

My personal example: Many years ago, when I was divorcing the father of my children, I took a mental-health leave of absence from work. I focused on therapy and healing. I had been in a deep depression for quite some time, and it took all of my energy to get up in the morning and get my children off to school before sitting around in a funk. I would attend my therapy, and just in time for my kids to come home, I would put on my happy face again, or so I thought.

This went on for a few months, and one weekend when my kids were at their dad's, I got up on a Saturday morning and said out loud: "Enough of this, I am not wasting another day being depressed by what someone else has decided. I am not doing it anymore." Of course, going through a divorce is not a one-way street. All sides contribute to the break-up, but for my side of it, I had had it. I called my boss and went back to work on the following Monday morning.

For the first time in a long time, I felt empowered to take my life back. Here I am, several decades later, and working hard to keep my new life intact. I am determined to do whatever it takes. Fighting the negative thoughts and actions are part of taking my life back. I focus on slowing down and being present, as I know from the universe that I am exactly where I am meant to be at this time.

That is not to say that there were not roadblocks or setbacks. Of course, there were, but I found that the sooner I got back to my "positive" routine, the better.

This is not to say that I ignore the negativity and go on pretending. No, I work it through my mind and consciously let it go. If it is still nagging at me the next week, I know I need to talk about it more and try letting go again, all the while filling in the gaps with positive vibes.

When I was at the treatment centre, someone said that recovery is sometimes about "faking it until you make it". This resonated with me. At first it felt phoney to smile when I didn't feel like it, but over time, I realized that my behaviour was changing—albeit in baby steps.

I am eternally grateful every day for the strength I have found to accept the things I cannot change and the courage to change the things I can. My practice of daily meditation strengthens that gratitude every single day.

Around this time, I had the opportunity to participate in some more course work created and taught by my Kundalini teacher. I decided to take on this new learning to expand my knowledge on mindfulness and calm. My intention as I started was to both calm down and allow things to happen as the universe intended and to be calmer in terms of rushed timeframes, which I have a tendency to do.

I learned about self-forgiveness, first of all identifying how I chastise myself. If I start to understand how I allow my mind to self-sabotage my efforts, then I can work to change it. I was noticing more and more how often I belittled myself with negative self-talk. For example, I wasn't a good enough friend/mother/sibling. I wasn't smart enough to try that new challenge. Then there was the imposter syndrome where I would put on my defensive air and think that I was fooling others. I knew that I was constantly questioning my abilities and over-analyzing why I couldn't accomplish something. It was stifling my life and dreams, and I knew it. If I live for another twenty years, was I going to live like this, degrading myself, seeing the negative, and generally seeing everything around me as a chore to live through?

My tendency to compare myself to others who are 'better' than me was getting tiresome, and I no longer wanted to live with this false story I loved to tell. I was starting to see that I needed to love and care for myself, and accept myself flaws and all; this is who I am. I recalled how often in my life I had said yes to others, when I knew deep down I wanted to say no. This applied to small tasks, but also to larger issues such as toxic relationships and, in my case, two failed marriages.

This was a powerful lesson, and I wanted to learn more. The doors were opening wider and wider. I could see that I used my addiction as a tool to ignore what I really wanted inside, and that I used drink as an escape from facing my pain. I could see that my pain was often self-inflicted as my negative self-talk kept me from standing tall and taking back my life. That had to change. Now that I had two years of sobriety under my belt, it was time to dig deeper.

I wanted to heal the empath within myself. From my journaling, the traits of an empath that I wrote were: *Perfectionist; need to control; people pleaser; lack of boundaries; too sensitive; anxious.*

Does any of this sound familiar? It sure did for me.

In the past when I heard the term "self-care", I thought of hygiene; not only cleansing of the physical body, but feeding and perhaps exercising the physical body. Now I was learning that there is also energy self-care, which I hadn't consciously considered in the past.

Some of the energy self-care notes I made for a list to go in my journal were:

- *Mindful eating with less processed and chemical food. Paying attention to how my body responds to different foods and making appropriate changes as needed.*
- *Mindful breathing. Actually sitting and being fully aware of my breathing. Using breath to calm myself. Deep breathing through*

the nose. My yoga practice teaches many types of breathing, such as alternate nose breathing, breath of fire, lion's breath, to name a few, all with different purposes.

- *Daily meditation. I have been doing this, but of course sometimes I run short of time during the day. However, I am learning that meditation can be done by sitting and listening to music, by walking, or during my gardening or sewing time. It didn't have to be me sitting and watching the screen and the teacher on Zoom. My husband says his meditation is often him walking or biking and taking in the sights and sounds around him.*

- *Stop and listen to the sounds around me—physical sounds that is. Listen more closely to what my intuition is telling me, and trust it. It has taken time to learn to listen to my intuition more closely, and it is still a work in progress.*

- *Look for activities that bring me joy or cause me to want to play. I discovered the new museum in Edmonton. I love going there, and this has sparked my interest in going to other cities' museums and learning.*

- *LAUGH out loud. It feels sooooo good.*

- *More movement including walking and my yoga. Note: I am not athletic at all, never enjoyed it, and remember skipping gym class in high school. So, needless to say this is a challenge for me, but again, a work in progress.*

- *Travel. Certainly Covid stopped most of that, but as things loosened up, we are able to travel a bit more, even if it is a trip in our own country where there is so much to offer.*

- *Consciously choosing good thoughts. I remember an old expression I learned years ago: "You get what you focus on." If you constantly focus on what you don't have, don't like, or what is not going well for you, well, guess what? You get more of it. So if I start focusing on what I do, love, and dream of, perhaps…. I know from experience that this works beautifully.*

- *Journal my thoughts and feelings. I have been doing that, but re-enforcement is great.*

These were powerful lessons. My journal started to be more powerful in my mind, as I read the list before writing and asked myself how I could incorporate these things into my day or week.

If you journal at the end of your day, ask yourself how you will incorporate some of the items on this list into your next day.

The Tenth Stair: Connection & Gratitude

Thank you. Thank you. Thank you.

—Cheryl

Let's talk about CONNECTION. I believe that you need some sort of connection to stay sober or clean. I know someone who has relapsed a number of times. She prefers to stay at home and work at her craft, which is painting. This sounds very relaxing to me, and I wish I had the talent. But what I see in her is her fear to go out and meet others. I have encouraged her to at least to go out and look at someone else's art work at a gallery or a festival. However, she wants to stay in her sanctuary of her creative world. From my perspective, I hope that one day she will find the courage to not only share her talent, but go out and be in awe of someone else's talent. Perhaps one day. If you read this, "Sandy", please think about expanding your world.

Make a connection with like-minded people who want the same for either themselves or for you—whether it be with a sponsor, a good friend, a relative, or a group. I met many people in rehab that were short of friends outside of their addiction, and therefore groups such as AA or NA were critical, as they could find like-minded people there. So, if you find yourself on this difficult set of stairs, ensure you have someone to connect with in the more trying times. I recently attended a celebration meeting from the treatment centre, and I was reminded, loud and clear, of the fellowship and connection that is in this community. Attending were those alumni, like me, who already know the value and comfort of being with community and like-minded people. Also, there were people still in treatment. I saw a few, appearing like deer in headlights, as I once was. I hope that by their attentiveness during the celebration that they were starting to see the value and feel the camaraderie.

As I mentioned earlier in this book, for my first year, I relied on the camaraderie and comfort of the Zoom meetings hosted by the treatment centre I attended. They were part of my "circle". As time went on, I branched off with smaller groups such as Just for Today. I also had many contacts with several individuals I knew from rehab, and we talked regularly. I was becoming more comfortable in telling people about my new way of life, and I found it easier to establish boundaries with good friends and family. I still work on it, but I feel that I am getting more comfortable in keeping boundaries.

For many reasons, I have had very few close friends in my life. Part of that was my lack of trust: trusting that others would have my back, that others truly cared, and that in times of need, they would be there for me. That trust faded as I grew older, and I was convinced that was just the way it was in life. You know, people in it only for themselves.... We all know a few!

There were a number of events in my early life where I felt totally alone and that I had no one to turn to or talk to. The first time I felt this was when I was about eleven years old. I can identify another time at sixteen years, then again at around twenty-five years of age. Each of these times are crystal clear in my mind, as if they were yesterday. In other words, I remember them in full-blown technicolour, slowly seeing myself backing away from people as time went on. I felt betrayed and abandoned, and the result was to deal with the events and the feelings around them by myself. I learned to be cautious of others and their motives, which was not a foundation for close friends. Later in life, I was betrayed by spouses as well, cementing what I believed all along. The specific events don't really matter at this point. The part that matters is how I learned from this foundation, albeit much later in life, and let those events go so that they no longer l actively live in my head. Hey, sometimes it takes a while!

I have a dear friend, Joanne, who I have known for over forty-five years. Throughout the years, we have lived in different cities, we have worked together, and we have worked for different firms. Our paths were similar in terms of divorcing the fathers of our children (we both had daughters), then raising our children as single parents. My point is that we connect. Over the years, we had periods of time when we rarely saw or talked with each other. This was not because we were arguing or angry with each other. Quite simply, our lives were hectic. We both were challenged with demanding careers and, of course, dealing with the challenges (many!) of raising our young girls. For those single parents out there, I am sure you can relate. In my mind, Joanne and I speak the same language. Whenever we re-connect, it feels like we saw each other yesterday. There is no slipping away from the friendship in troubled times.

What I know in my heart is that regardless of the connection I may feel with a good friend, or a family member, or even a partner, I have to care for myself first so that I am whole for others. That was the case when I went to the treatment centre. I did it for ME. I did not go to treatment for my friends, including my dear husband or for my daughters. I went to treatment for myself so I could be a better human and, in turn, a better spouse, mother, and friend. I went to treatment to finally find and embrace the root causes of my addiction to ensure 100% success in recovery.

For me, true connection with a friend is when I feel seen, I feel heard, and I feel valued with that person. Hold on to this type of relationship. It is rare and is meant to be cherished.

Surround yourself with people who, when you are doing well, don't want to blow out your candle. If they do, consider this: *"I thought she'd be a good friend, but she is a candle-blower-outer."* Then, move on. That would have been a valuable lesson for me decades ago!

You may also discover, as I did, that some friends (or working colleagues or relatives) may back away from this new person named YOU. I recognized this happening a number of times as I started sharing my experiences with others. At first, I thought my old colleagues from work no longer wanted to be associated with me because I was a bad enough drinker that I had to go to an addiction treatment centre. After all, if I could handle my drink, I wouldn't need to do that, right? Perhaps I was now seen as "one of those people".

I would like to define what I mean by "one of those people". Think back to the talk around the water cooler about the new person. "I heard that she was fired from her last job"; "I heard that he harassed someone in the workplace"; "I heard she goes out drinking every weekend, and that's why she is often late on Monday mornings"; "I heard her spouse takes drugs." On and on and on and on. Perhaps this is what was happening.

The same things happen with the "nosey neighbours" or the excluded family member. I am sure you also know people who make inappropriate comments about people of a different culture, race, or economic background. If they do that, then your addiction transformation would make for "prime" gossip.

It is true that some neighbours, friends, family members, or co-workers will judge you for your behaviour, instead of celebrating your taking action to solve the issue. They may take it so far as to cut you out of their lives. Or, perhaps even worse, ignore you, and use your situation as "the juicy hot topic" of the week. For whatever reason, probably our own insecurities, we humans judge other humans who are different than us, and backing away is one of the "solutions".

But—and this is a BIG BUT—it may also be true that those neighbours, friends, family, or co-workers are not judging you. It could be they are simply moving on in their lives, just like you are. It could also be true that they are in awe of your accomplishment and secretly proud of your work, and just don't know how to express it. Perhaps, they are no longer an energetic match for you at this stage, and that is okay.

On the other hand, they may choose to stay at a distance, as they are nervous about facing their own demons. My demons were masked by alcohol. Some people's demons are masked by seclusion, depression, or suicide. Some demons are masked by drugs, inappropriate sexual behaviour, eating disorders, or perhaps raging anger or other forms of violence. Some are coping with demons, and the way they deal with them is to find fault in others.

There are far too many people in our world, including in your own backyard that did not have support in terms of counselling, rehabilitation, family and close friends and are now begging on the street and/or have lost their families or are homeless.

The bottom line is that you do not know another's circumstances, so lay off the judgements and show some empathy for a fellow member of the universe. Support them if you can. There are many ways to give back, which I will talk about later in this book.

Similarly, you do not know why people react the way they do to your situation. Those around you may never accept your new way of life. I have heard the phrase many times of late: "Perhaps they are no longer an energetic match for you."

This can be hard to face, but it is also okay. We as humans are constantly evolving, at least physically as we age, and for many, emotionally as well. This is YOUR LIFE to live.

Put it out to the universe that you are seeking like-minded people to join your "tribe" (your circle of friends/supporters) and be grateful for them coming into your life.

What do I mean by "putting it out in the universe"? For some, that may be prayer with your higher power (God, Goddess, Allah, Buddha, Creator, Nature, Spirit Guides, your recovery group—AA or NA, Mother Earth, as examples). For some, it may be meditation or mindfulness. It may also include talking to people and asking for help. It may be talking to the stars and asking to connect to someone who knows your journey. It also could mean asking those spirits that are in your corner—maybe a deceased friend, spouse, or parent.

Whatever form it takes, reach out as much as you are capable of at this time. I was recently in a favourite bookstore and shared with an associate of the shop that I was writing. That emerged into a larger conversation about addiction, and both of us sharing a bit about our stories. I later found out that she is the manager of that bookstore and is connected with a writing friend of mine who regularly does book signings at that location. You just never know what connections you will find out there in the world. You will probably marvel at how small the world is when you realize the connection.

Speaking of small worlds, I am going to pause here to tell you a story of "what a small world it is". My husband and I have known each other for over forty years. His spouse, Gail, was a dear friend of mine. We worked together, and through that connection, I also got to know her husband over the years. A while after Gail's passing, Roger and I would go for lunch or a coffee, and as time went on, we became a couple.

The first time we took a trip together, we went to Vancouver Island, specifically Victoria among other destinations. I had a favourite uncle who lived there in a seniors' home, and I wanted to visit with him before we headed home. As we walked through the parking lot on our way to visit my Uncle George, my husband asked me about him so that he would have conversation bits to talk to him about.

As it turned out, my uncle and Roger's father, Ray, who had passed, worked for the same company back in the day. Not only that, but they both worked in the Human Resources field…interesting coincidence. Later when Roger and my uncle were sharing their stories, it turned out that Roger's father and mother were best of friends with my aunt and uncle. The conversation turned to Uncle George's memories of BBQ's in their backyard with all of their children (a.k.a. Roger and his siblings with my cousins). What are the chances?

Back to the reasons why people may drift away from you. Consider the possibility that people drift away because they don't know how to "handle" you anymore in terms of what to say, or for that matter, what to do. For example, they may wonder if they can ask you about your journey, or if that would upset you. They may wonder if they can still order a drink at a restaurant even though you are not drinking. Or, perhaps, they may recognize that they too need some help and aren't ready to face it yet, so backing off from you is somewhat easier.

We humans are really good at ignoring what we don't want to hear, aren't we? In this case, you may have opened a door a little crack, and you will be in their mind. If and when they decide to start this freeing journey, they may call and ask to connect. In one case for me, a friend asked the details about rehab as they had a brother who was suffering. Someone else, when hearing my journey, said that they should probably cut back themselves. Did they? I have no idea, and it is not my business. If they have more questions, I am sure they will connect with me.

When I first considered taking action on my addiction, I knew no one who had made or were on this journey. I wish I had. It is likely I do know someone, but they haven't made it public. I wanted to make this public, and hence, writing this book. I want to put out there in the universe this how-to guide to Pure Joy and hope that people will reach out, if not directly, then to a friend or family member in their circle who is seeking Joy.

It took me a while to learn this, but as time went on, I found that I became more comfortable in sharing my journey when asked about why I was not partaking.

In the first few years, I would just say I wasn't drinking for health purposes. Now, I am more comfortable in expanding on this by saying things like: "I went to addiction rehabilitation, and am working hard at my continued sobriety, so please know that I will no longer be serving alcohol in my home." "Although I am no longer drinking, feel free to order yourself an alcoholic drink in the restaurant." "As you know, I am no longer drinking, but I find it still triggering, so if you wouldn't mind, can we all just enjoy some lemonade instead."

The full story is not necessary for most situations. Only you will know what works for you. If a friend is not willing to comply with your request, perhaps they are not as close a friend as you thought they were.

Some time ago, I went to a dinner theatre with three other women. One offered me a glass of wine, and I said no, and at the time, I was quite comfortable in saying I no longer drink. This was followed by inquiries as to if this was for health reasons. I said yes for health, but feeling totally comfortable with this person, I further expanded on the reasons. I told her about my journey to rehab and my continued journey to remain sober. I was comforted that she was very supportive. Know that during your own journey, it won't always turn out positively like this interaction did.

There are those in my life who will learn for the first time, while reading this memoir, what life has been about for Cheryl. It is not like I took out advertising on a billboard, nor should you. I play it by ear, knowing that sometimes a situation just lends itself to "the" conversation, and I take advantage of that. There are some people in my life I only see in a social setting, and doing this at a house party or BBQ probably isn't the place. It is your life and your comfort level, so take it easy on yourself and do what works for you at the time. I will say that having your story out in the open is easier and more natural, as you don't have to worry about slipped words or awkward moments. Take the time you need; only you know when that is.

If the reason you are reading this is not because you are climbing the stairs out of addiction, but rather looking to live a more satisfying life, then telling people is not really necessary. People will start to "see" you differently. They will see you radiating and wonder what you are doing, and then you get to share the Joy with another human being!

So, let's talk about GRATITUDE a little more. I thank the universe every day for the friends and family I have who support me. For me, expressing gratitude is not just for the obvious things—like having a roof over my head, having a job when so many do not, or when thanking someone for a card or a gift. For me, it is also feeling gratitude for the things we don't think about specifically, or we take for granted. For example: I am grateful I am breathing without difficulty; I am grateful for clean water to drink; I am grateful for my continued good health; I am grateful to live in a country like Canada and not in a war zone; I am grateful for my spouse, my children, my family, my friends, etc.; I am grateful I have the resources to help another fellow human being.

I don't know what tomorrow will bring, so I try to take time every day to pause and express my gratitude. Here is a short writing by Lauren Oliver, a contributor to *Everyday Mindfulness—365 Ways to a Centred Life*, the book that I mentioned earlier:

> *Maybe you can afford to wait. Maybe for you there's a tomorrow. Maybe for you there's one thousand tomorrows, or three thousand, or ten. Perhaps you have so much time you can bathe in it, roll around it, let it slide like coins through your fingers. Maybe you feel that you have so much time left in your life that you can waste it. But for some of us, there's only today. And the truth is, you never really know.*

Or consider Groucho Marx's words:

> *Each morning when I open my eyes, I say to myself: I, not events, have the power to make me happy or unhappy today. I can choose which it shall be. Yesterday is dead, tomorrow hasn't arrived yet. I have just one day, today, and I'm going to be happy in it.*

Being consciously grateful every day takes practice. It may take some time to get into the habit of mindfully being grateful and expressing it. As you attempt this, you will find yourself slipping into old conversations and old thoughts, but as soon as you realize it: Stop, re-group, and try again. You may consider making this a part of your routine to stay clean/sober/addiction-free. If addiction is not a problem in your life, that is fabulous, but being mindful and grateful every day is a joyous way to live.

It could be part of your wake-up routine. Get up, make the bed, brush your teeth, and express your gratitude to the world as you plan out your day. For others, my husband included, it may be the end of the day that works best for expressing your gratitude for the specifics of the day. As Roger will tell you, every night as he is settling into sleep, he says a short prayer of thanks for his day.

The bottom line is that morning, noon, night, every day, every week ... it is up to you. I reinforce daily what I am trying to achieve in my life at this time. As you are aware, I journal daily, so it becomes a part of that routine.

Perhaps journaling has not been part of your life, or doesn't feel like a fit for you. That's okay. There are many resources out there about being, acting, and practicing gratitude. If this conscious effort at being grateful is not currently part of your daily life, start small. If you are keeping a journal, make a part of each journal entry a sentence or two on what you are grateful for. Another option could be to keep a pad of paper on the kitchen table, nightstand, or beside the remote, for that matter, and jot a few words of thanks down. Or make it simple and just say the words out loud as you take a walk. It really does not matter, but you will find more joy when you express joy for your current life and circumstance. Baby steps will eventually turn into climbing steep stairs.

Instead of cursing about the slow grocery check-out person, perhaps express to yourself your gratitude that you are able to afford the food you are buying. Speeding up in the cue at the grocery store is not going to make your day that much different, so calm down!

Instead of honking your horn at the cautious driver ahead of you, perhaps say to yourself, "Maybe they are having an upsetting day," or "Maybe they are just learning to drive." Another possibility is that they are a senior near the end of their driving time and are a bit slower and cautious. Cursing or honking your horn at the driver does not get you to your destination any faster, and it only adds to your sad, frustrated day. Regardless, I am grateful that my day today is pretty good even if it is not the best day for another person.

When I get frustrated, I try to stop myself and find the positive side of the situation I find myself in. But this doesn't always work for me. Why you ask? Because I am human, and as such, I make mistakes or overreact just like you do at times. But with practice, you will find it becomes easier. Start noticing the tiny changes in your life. Those small changes add up to larger changes. Take notice of yourself. If you think you are not making enough progress towards living a more joyful life, consider the following memory of mine.

Many years ago, when I was in therapy, my counsellor suggested that I was only focusing on the negative side of my life. Of course,

I argued that point because, after all: I was overwhelmed at work, I was struggling being a new single mother, I was angry with my soon to be ex-husband, the lawyers were wrong, the system was wrong, and on top of all that, I was continually running out of time. Everything and everyone around me were wrong, and of course, this was not my fault. Yeah, right!

The counsellor patiently listened and gave me some coloured index cards to carry with me along with a pen. My task was to make a list on the cards of all that I had accomplished that day—nothing but. It didn't matter how small the accomplishment. So, I did it. The list seemed silly at first as I jotted down some mundane tasks, but eventually I saw the value.

Some of the things on the list, now that I was on my own with my girls, were small things like phoning the utility companies to make the bills in my name alone; getting my own credit card; changing my married name back to my maiden name; signing the final papers, and on and on. Trivial, you ask? No, I say. I needed to help myself see that I was making headway on my list that had been spinning in my brain, keeping me agitated, and robbing me of my sleep.

The therapist was getting me to realize that I was making some progress on what seemed to be a never-ending list. I also realized that often I was doing what I call busy work: those tasks that don't matter, but I felt obligated to do. Does the universe really care if my laundry is done once a week, not twice? Is it okay to just relax and breathe and sit in a bath for a while? Will I get reprimanded if I don't cook tonight, but rather order a pizza? If it does truly matter, to whom? A lot of busy work is not necessary, and we do it out of habit, or because that was how we were taught. In my case, I was taught by my mom, who was a stay-at-home parent. For me, working at a full-time job meant that some things had to be let go of—either all together or cut back.

If you take the time to write down what you are grateful for, you will be surprised that the list is endless. The more grateful I become, the more I am appreciative of my continued journey in my sobriety and my life in general.

As the day draws to an end, find yourself a quiet space and write a list of everything you have achieved today. Think of moments, not miracles. There will be days that your to-do list looks like the next page of this book...and that is perfect!

TODAY'S TO-DO LIST

inhale

exhale

inhale

exhale

inhale

exhale

inhale

exhale

inhale

exhale

inhale

exhale

inhale

exhale

Go ahead and mark that last page to recall this to-do list, and don't feel guilty for it. How about taking a picture of this page and putting it front and centre on your workspace or on the fridge?

You are a deserving human who is doing your best to navigate this world. Don't forget that!

There was a book many years ago called *Don't Sweat the Small Stuff...and It's All Small Stuff* by Richard Carlson. This book was written in 1997 and was in so many homes and businesses. I remember buying a few copies and sending them as gifts to friends, relatives, and colleagues. So many years later, this expression of not sweating the small stuff is still prevalent in everyday conversation, and the books are still readily available.

Richard was a husband and father, when he died at forty-five years old of a pulmonary embolism while on a flight, as part of a book promotion tour in 2006. As I have said a number of times in this book, you just never know what tomorrow will bring. He was at the top of his writing career, and in a flash, he was gone at forty-five years old.

When you are fighting and/or recovering from addiction and learning to cope better with your life, you may find it overwhelming to add routines into your life such as meetings, exercise, therapy, etc. These new tasks do take time, but your recovery is important time, and the rest of the tasks can take a back seat. I made a point of restructuring my day to include time for meditation, as an example. I know people that never miss their walk or their trip to the gym. It is about your priorities, not someone else's.

You can vacuum again today for pet hair, or do it once a week and leave it at that so that you can attend your recovery meeting in person or online. The pet hair will wait until you do your yoga practice or jog around the block, if that is your thing.

Other days you may skip the vacuum all together, because at this point, you realize that your sobriety is number one in your life now. You are number one in your life, and that's all there is to it. Make YOU and your recovery a number-one priority. In this story, the vacuum is the "small stuff", if you hadn't gathered that by now!

Another point I have realized about gratitude is that the more you give, the more you receive. If you are having a great day, and all is flowing smoothly, consider making a great day for someone else. This can be as simple as smiling and wishing another well. This could be paying it forward by buying the coffee for the person behind you in the drive-through. I used to drink an Iced Capp from Tim's on the way to work every day, and I loved doing this! This could be complimenting someone else on their achievement, demeanour, or a job well done.

Currently, I am working on "making someone else's day". Examples of late: letting another car in ahead of me as I am driving; taking a few minutes to chat with a senior sitting by himself in the coffee shop; picking up a second box of food in the store and donating it to the food bank; sending a random postcard (yes, a postcard) to someone I haven't spoken to in a while; thanking someone or a group for their contribution or service. Recently, I picked up a huge fruit tray and dropped it off at the local fire station to thank them for all they do. There are so many examples that will not only brighten someone else's experience, but you will discover it also brightens yours. Going for a walk? Why not make a point of smiling and saying hello to everyone you encounter today? So what, if they don't respond? So few people do this that some may be at a loss for words when you greet them. The feeling inside that will fill you up when you give back is fabulous!

I have found that giving back and expressing your gratitude will strengthen your inner peace. That is, it will enhance your gratitude for yourself and your progress in making a better life. It will also strengthen your gratitude for others and their contribution to your inner peace and joy. As the Dalai Lama said: *"Do not let the behaviour of others destroy your inner peace."*

You are working hard on your quest to find a more fulfilling life, so don't let anyone belittle your efforts. Don't let anyone tease or ridicule you for some of the pieces of your journey. Know that your increased inner joy and peace will give you the kind of life for which you will be grateful at the end of your days. I personally want to know that, at the end of my life, I have left all of my cards on the table: that I have done all I wanted or dreamed of and that I no longer harbour regrets or resentments towards anyone or anything.

I continue every day to work on what brings me joy, and no one can take that away from me. I may not like what you have said or done, and it may upset me, but I will still hold on to my joy and no one can alter that. End of Story. Period.

The Eleventh Stair: Giving Back

*If you don't love yourself, you cannot love others.
If you have no compassion for yourself,
you cannot develop compassion for others.*

—Dalai Lama

It has been re-enforced to me throughout my journey that my joy and contentment in life is expanded when I am giving back. I know it gives me joy and a warm, fuzzy feeling in my tummy! I also know that when I remove a large part of my mind that is occupied with worry, anger, resentment, negativity, etc., there is more room for joy in my mind or heart.

A pastor said to me once: "Don't let all the negativity and worry take up a parking space in your brain. Allow the positivity and joy to park there instead." It makes me laugh and whenever I think of this example, I literally see Karen, the pastor, in the parking lot she said this to me!

During the first year or so of my recovery, my main focus was giving back to myself. After all, I had not been taking care of my physical body, let alone my mind. I had been isolating from the outside world more than normal. I was not eating properly either. With not taking care of me, how could I truly give to those around me? I couldn't, but now I could. I was consciously following my recovery routine of meetings, counselling, connecting with my addiction community, and daily hygiene (diet, exercise, grooming, etc.).

I was also ensuring that I followed my daily meditation, yoga, and journaling commitments to myself. I was not worried about this looking selfish on my part. I knew that I had to be whole first. I knew I had to love myself first. Only then could I consider others. If you have been on an airplane, as most have, you have heard the instruction to put on your oxygen mask first before helping others with theirs. This applies here and is called **self-care**.

This is in direct contrast to how some of my generation grew up. Looking after me first would have been seen by my parents or other elders as selfish or self-centred. At least that's how I interpreted it during most of my young years. Certainly, my mom in particular gave back to her community in many ways. She and Dad lived in a small community in Southern Ontario that was surrounded by fresh produce farms. I recall many times she and I would go berry picking and return home to make jam. On other occasions, we were buying cucumbers and making pickles. No matter what, half of the jars were reserved for the church sales. By the way, the church sale preserves got the fancy labels! She was also a crafty person and made decorations for the church bizarre. She was a talented maker and designer of stained glass, and I am sure she gave more away than she ever sold.

It was the "looking after yourself first" that may not have been my mom's normal, as it wasn't mine. Even when I was working full time, if I was asked to take something on outside of working hours, it was always at the sacrifice of my private time. This was mostly because of my people-pleasing trait and not wanting to let others down. For me now, it is about balance. It is not to say it is always "me first", but I work on saying no, if it is beyond my capacity at the time, rather than automatically agreeing to assist. I can't do and be all to everyone and neither can you. I suppose I thought I was Superwoman back in the day, but I definitely was not, and don't strive to be her anymore!

I want to address giving back in the form of entertaining and/or socializing. Alcohol in my house, particularly while entertaining, was the norm. Even when we hosted a larger group, I always provided plenty of food and beverage, including alcohol. Pretty much all of the time, inviting others over in the evening involved an alcoholic beverage of some sort.

It had been quite a long time since I invited family or friends to my home for an afternoon or a meal, mostly due to my not being comfortable in expressing my new norm. I wanted to resume hosting, particularly with friends and family who had been supporting my journey. It wasn't until about year two that I was feeling comfortable and wanted to start to reciprocate some invites.

DO WHAT IS RIGHT FOR YOU. If you are not ready for this stage, delay it. Just be sure to be honest with yourself as to why you are not wanting company either in your home or at an event. You just want to ensure that you are not reverting back to self-isolation, which by this stage, you realize is dangerous for sustained recovery.

My advice is to start slow and safe. Starting with twenty people over for Thanksgiving might be over the top. I knew that I wasn't ready for the stress that brings to me. I started with having a couple over for tea and cookies, or just a couple of family members over for a meal or BBQ. It was manageable, and it was setting myself up for success.

You may never return to the large gatherings of the past, and that's okay. Actually, Covid helped with this, and as it is still kicking around here and there, we are all a bit more cautious in terms of crowds. In my past, those entertainment days were full of fun and camaraderie. For me, that also meant attending the company Christmas party or picnic and being one of the last to leave with a taxi chit. There was always plenty of liquor, and that is no more, so times have changed for us. The lesson here is to do what works for you and your immediate family. This is a new way of living for some—certainly it was for me—and that may take some adjustments.

Yes, there were people who we now see less often, and at times, the invites don't seem to come as frequently, but that is okay with my husband and I. We see it as learning the grace of letting go and the power of moving forward!

You may find, as I did, that giving back to the neighbourhood, or another community that you used to be involved in, fell by the wayside during the height of your addiction or during Covid. Perhaps you never considered giving back to the community around you. If this is new to you, again, start out small and build from there. The satisfaction and pride in doing this is worth the effort. In my mind, giving back is not just about giving money or items. It is also about giving time.

One community that many in recovery consider giving back to is the addiction community: assisting with AA or NA meetings. Many of these communities put on events for their members such as BBQ's and other get-togethers. It may be time spent on the phone with a fellow recovering addict during a time of need, or just checking in with each other.

Look up volunteering in your city on the Internet, and you are likely to see all kinds of events. Perhaps start with the one-off events vs. a weekly commitment, and see how that works for you. If you are more of a homebody, maybe creating something to give away is more up your alley. For example, I knit thirty-five hats one winter to give to various charities. The following winter I made 5 quilts to donate. I try to always pick up an extra can of food at the grocery store and drop it in the donation bin on my way out. Growing veggies in your garden? Save some for a soup kitchen. Do you have an apple tree? Pick the excess to donate to the church ladies who make pies to sell, or to give to the food bank. There are many ways to give back, and it sure feels good. It will give you as much joy as the receiver feels.

Here is an interesting story that I read some time ago, on social media, and kept as a reminder. Many have put this story on SM, from many different countries, so the original author is unclear. However, the lesson is powerful and many postings suggest passing this valuable lesson along to others, as we can all learn from it.

Picture a very frail and elderly gentleman sitting at the edge of the outdoor market selling his eggs. He is probably about ninety years of age, and it is his practice to take time after rising every morning to go out to his chicken coup and collect eggs to sell, which supplements his income. His clothing is quite worn, as affording a new set of clothing is beyond his reach. He misses his long-time spouse, who was by his side for over sixty-five years.

On Tuesday morning, he was once again set up to sell his eggs, and a well-dressed woman came along and asked the old seller how much his eggs cost. He replied, "It's 25¢ per egg, Madam."

She turned to him and stated, "I will take six eggs for $1.25, not a penny more or I will leave."

The old seller replied, "Come take them at the price you want. Maybe this is a good beginning because I have not been able to sell even a single egg today." She took the eggs and walked away, feeling that she had won and proud of her negotiating skills.

She got into her fancy car and went to a posh restaurant where she was meeting her friend after shopping. While there, they ordered full lunches. They ended up eating little and left a fair bit on the plates. She then went to pay the bill. The bill cost her $45, and she gave the owner of the restaurant a $50 bill and told him to keep the change.

This incidence might seem quite normal to the owner, but very painful to the egg seller. The point is, why do we always show we have the power when we buy from needy people? And why are we more generous with those who do not even need the generosity? My father used to buy simple goods from poor people at high prices, even though he did not need them. Sometimes he even used to pay extra for them. I got concerned by this act and asked him why he did this. My father replied, *"It is a charity wrapped with dignity, my child."*

I believe this story says a lot about giving back, and it is one I attempt to live up to.

The Twelfth Stair: Focus & Curiosity

Everything is falling together perfectly, even though it looks as if some things are falling apart. Trust the process you are now experiencing.

—Neale Donald Walsch,
American Author of Conversations With God

Staying the course can be difficult. If you are looking for pure Joy, you need to practise keeping on track. Think of an athlete in professional sports. They practise their craft every day to get better and better at it. A friend recently said she was learning to golf. She said, "You don't become a master overnight, it takes practise. When you get frustrated, take a break, but don't give up."

Recovery is no different. I have a daughter who is a runner. She started with smaller five-kilometre races and progressed to ten-kilometre runs. Having accomplished that level, she then started registering for half marathons, and then full marathons, and currently ultra-races. Running is a large part of her life. As I prepare this book for publishing, she just posted a note on Instagram about running her forty-fifth marathon in her forty-fifth year. To keep on that path takes discipline, training, and hard work.

Over time, I knew that I had to consciously focus on my recovery until such time that it would start to pay off in terms of not having to "work" at it consciously as much and become my "normal" or natural way of living. I have to keep sobriety in the forefront of my mind, of course. I am not running a race (in fact not running at all!), but I try every day to stay focused on my climbing of the stairs. Over the course of the past three years, I notice regularly that I am seeing some aspect of my world around me differently.

When I was a young child, as for most young ones, I was curious about things. I recall living in a particular house on a street called MacDonnell Street. My family lived in that house until I was about eight years old. I had some friends down the street, and we played together almost every day. We would pretend and play "teacher" at times, or other times, we would play the "mother". The memory that sticks in my brain was a particular day when my friend and I were playing outside, and it started to rain. We were playing under the cover of her house carport. The rain was heavy, the kind that is audible as it hits the ground. We heard the crack of thunder and lightning, and the sky was quite dark. At some point, we noticed that it was not raining across the street. "How can that be?" we asked each other. We had another friend across the street, and we called across at each other about the strange scene. We started running back and forth across the street, delighting in the fact that Leslie's house was dry and our side of the street was teeming with water!

This fascinated me, and when my dad returned from work, I was excited to ask him how this could be possible. How could it rain on one side of MacDonnell Street and not the other? He told me that God didn't know where the streets started and ended when He sent the raindrops. It was us as humans who decided where the streets were. That was not God's decision. It fascinated me, and this example demonstrates the curiosity of children.

We all grew up in different environments, which shaped who we have become today. Some of us grew up in a household with a mom and dad, some in a single-parent household, and some in a home with two moms or two dads. Perhaps your parents both worked, and you got to understand what it was like in a daycare or after-school environment. Perhaps one parent stayed home and was always there to greet you at the end of your day. Your home may have been peaceful, or it may have been tense or even abusive.

You may have had the opportunity to finish high school and move onto higher education. In contrast, perhaps you were not able to complete even a basic education due to circumstances in your home. Perhaps in your early teens, you had to quit school to help with the family business/farm. In time, you went to work—perhaps in a lifelong career or moving from job to job, trying to find your passion. Maybe finding passion in your work was never a thought, as it was all about making enough money to survive.

Some of us had children, and maybe even grandchildren. Some never did find a life partner and live alone. Some of these circumstances were forced upon us, some were choices our parents made, and some are choices we made for ourselves.

My point is that whatever your circumstances are now, you were shaped by what you have already lived through—good, bad, or indifferent. To spend your adult life moaning about what you did or didn't have is a waste of time. It is done, and now, the question is: How are you going to live differently?

Apparently, we are all born with curiosity. Little ones are always asking questions of adults, wanting to know why, where, how long, etc. "Are we there yet?" "But why, Mom?" "Where does the sun go to sleep?" "Why does the sun come up?" "Why is the grass green and not purple?"

As time goes on, children go to school and learn answers as taught by their teachers, according to the local curriculum. In order to complete the standard learnings by the end of the term, there is pressure to finish the work and reward the child for finishing vs. rewarding the child for their thought-provoking questions.

In addition, the number of firsts for a young person starts to diminish and, therefore, the questions do as well. Imagine the delight of a child seeing a rainbow for the first time, and the questions that would emerge about this new sight. How did that rainbow get into the sky? Who painted the colours in the sky? Why wasn't there a rainbow today? As time goes on, after seeing many rainbows, that child hardly notices them anymore and doesn't ask any more questions. The curiosity about rainbows is no longer.

I think I was about nine or ten years of age and attending a summer camp when I first saw the Northern Lights dancing over Nelson Lake in Ontario. I clearly recall my total fascination and curiosity about this "cool new thing" and a group of fellow campers and myself bombarding the director of the camp (Mr. Nyhill, as I recall) with questions. This discovery from childhood was both fun and memorable.

At the same time, we as children were being read fantasy and fairy-tale books, which filled our excited brains with delight. We probably dreamt of the possibilities of being a princess, a mermaid, an astronaut landing on the moon or Mars, or a superhero like Spiderman. However, as these exciting times start to fade, and we become caught up in the "real" world, we start to lose our dreams about our future, and in some cases, our confidence.

When I was around eight or nine years old, my parents put me on the train in our small Northern Ontario community to go to Toronto. My Grannie Cherry lived there. I was a big girl now going on the train by myself. The train, the porters on the train, the scenery along the way were exciting and new. I am sure if there was a photo of me then that my eyes would have been as large as saucers. I was also probably full of butterflies in my tummy. That week was full of new and fun activities and learnings. When I arrived, my grannie had knitted a whole bunch of outfits for my doll, and I remember thinking it was Christmas again.

But what was I most excited about? I knew that Grannie Cherry was going to take me to my first movie at a big theatre. I probably sat in the theatre with my mouth gaped open while watching the larger-than-life Julie Andrews and Dick Van Dyke dance to "Supercalifragilisticexpialidocious" in the movie *Mary Poppins*. I loved that song and delighted in learning all the words! That day, I vividly remember thinking that I wanted to be Mary when I grew up. The curiosity and excitement of children, which fades as we grow older, needs to be consciously worked on so we can revive it in ourselves.

For me, I first learned fear in my last elementary year. We had just moved to the big city of Toronto, and I was teased mercifully in the playground by a couple of class bullies. The curriculum was different than I was used to, and I wasn't understanding it. But my curiosity was melting, as I was afraid that asking questions would mean repercussions at recess. I was even afraid to tell my parents about what was happening at school. I knew that my dad had gotten a promotion and that was why we moved, and I didn't want him or my mom to know I was struggling. I was a people-pleaser even back then.

As we get older, we get preoccupied with learning how to find our way in the world. We may attend higher education and spend time trying to figure out what vocation we want to pursue, while learning how to survive adult life without parents looking after us. Our curiosity fades as we focus on the material world, making a living, buying our first car or home, and generally keeping up with the Joneses as they say. Some would say we are busy staying upright on the treadmill of life.

I certainly knew I was guilty of the perpetual to-do list, the decreasing energy of not getting it all done, and the pressures of society to have "enough". I always felt an additional pressure of being a single, working mom. Abundance to me at that time was mostly about "stuff" acquired. It was about moving towards being mortgage-free, having a reliable and nice car, and perhaps a few vacations thrown in. It was not about the full scope of what abundance means to me today.

I am staying focused on being curious through this journey of mine. Staying curious means keeping my mind active and open. By having my mind open, I am able to focus on my pathway. I work on being open to new ideas, new challenges, and breaking down my pre-conceived ideas about many aspects of life. I am also aware of letting go of aspects of my life that no longer work for me: activities, people, routines, and relationships that just don't fill me up any longer, and in many cases hold me back from the pure joy I am seeking.

At the time of this writing, I am about to embark on a six-month journey with my Kundalini teacher along with five other powerhouse women. In preparation for this amazing adventure, a course called Chrysalis, I decided to devote my meditations to dreaming the "impossible" and finding ways to make the imagined a reality. For a child, this probably would come naturally without a thought. For me, it is a learning process to dream the impossible dream. See the back of the book for contact information.

Abundance for me is no longer about keeping up with the Joneses or acquiring something bigger/better. Today my definition of abundance means mindfulness focusing on joy. I was learning (and still am) about slowing down my thoughts. This meant not chastising myself for not having checked all the boxes. I was learning to trade the number of tick marks on my list for looking for and experiencing new things and being more curious. I want to ask the child-like questions without being childish.

I believe that part of the reason we turn off our curiosity is that, as we get older, we gain experience, knowledge, and wisdom. For some, that means knowing all the answers and believing we are always right, and that it is our way or the highway, as the expression goes. I know of many people, as I am sure you do, who are proud of knowing it all. You will recognize them when their sentences start with, "Back in my day, it was better because…" or "When I was a kid, we talked to people. We didn't text people. We visited people instead of watching their lives on social media," and on and on. Exhausting!

I want to trade in the never-ending lists of what I should do, and do more of what I want to do. I want to spend more time learning new things instead of defending the old. This is part of unravelling the quest to find more joy in my life.

There are literally thousands of books out there to reference on finding more joy. Here are a few paths that resonate with me.

More Pathways to Joy

Reading Books: I love to read and almost always have a fiction book on the go. This has been the case for as long as I remember. The change is that I now always have two books on the go. The fiction book is for general entertainment. The other is for learning. A fun read vs. learning read. A more serious book takes more time. I generally read a chapter or two at a sitting, along with my highlighter and post-it tabs. I enjoy taking the time to really absorb the new concept or idea and how it may or may not pertain to my life.

At the time of this writing, I am reading *Living Untethered: Beyond the Human Predicament* by Michael Singer. This book was preceded by *The Untethered Soul: The Journey Beyond Yourself* by the same author. I often journal after reading a chapter or two, capturing my learnings and my thoughts of how it applies to me. I generally read several fun fiction books in a month and only one serious book over the course of a month or two.

Cultural Events: Year-round, there are many festivals and cultural events held around the city I live in. The Asian Festival, the Heritage Festival, and the Indigenous market are a few examples that I have recently noticed popping up around the city. Learning about someone else's upbringing, culture, and unique traditions is not about adapting to the ways of others. It is about educating ourselves to end up with a deeper understanding. For me, a deeper understanding lends itself to less judgement and more appreciation.

Travel: I have been fortunate over the years to have travelled to other countries. Let me share a story that I experienced once while in Bali, Indonesia. I learned a lot about not only the religions of Bali, such as Hinduism, but also about the Balinese people's way of life. Every person I met during each of my trips to this country was happy, full of joy, and grateful for all that was around them.

While visiting once, my husband and I admired a painting in a shop, and we wanted to purchase it. We called out for someone to help us, and it appeared no owner was around the shop. This was a "fancy" shop with a real floor versus a dirt floor. Knowing that people in Ubud usually had their home behind the shop, we called out past the gate to find the shop keeper, but to no avail. We went to the shop next door to enquire, and the shop owner said that the gallery owners were attending temple and should be back within the hour.

We returned later and got chatting with the family that owned the gallery. We asked about the fact that their shop was wide open earlier and if they were worried about theft while they were out. The puzzled look on the owner's face spoke a thousand words. He replied very frankly and said that no, they were not worried, as that would be the thief's karma, not theirs that would be affected.

What a trusting culture, which is in such contrast to our North American ways.

After Covid, we travelled more in our own country and discovered so much about our own backyard. We are blessed to live in a country like Canada, particularly with our cultural diversity and freedoms.

Another way that we travel is by exploring our local museums and galleries. When in other cities around our nation, we have now started to explore other cities' offerings in this regard, and thoroughly find joy in that.

Protests: A friend in BC suggested attending protests—either as a participant or to learn by talking to the participants to try and understand their viewpoint. I thought this was an interesting activity, particularly in reference to environmental issues versus pipelines and the future of our environment in general. Talking to someone who has a different view is not to say you will change your mind. What it will do is broaden your mind.

On perhaps a gentler note, instead of a protest, attend gatherings where political speeches or events hosted by a political leader take place. Perhaps even volunteer with a candidate. Taking the time to understand the other party is healthy. I know many people who vote for the same party for a lifetime, because that's what their parents did, and therefore, they don't listen or hear new ideas and approaches.

Some of these ideas may seem strange as a pathway to more joy, but for me, better understanding and less judgement brings me more joy.

Recently I heard that Ed Sheeran, singer/writer of the modern age, turned off all electronics in pursuit of more joy and creativity. When I heard this, I was reminded of walking recently on Vancouver Island with my friend. Yes, we were chatting at times, but mostly I was walking, taking in the beauty of the nature around me, listening to the sounds of nature, and feeling peaceful.

As I moved along the pathway, I saw a few other walkers, who were madly texting on their phones and missing out on the best part! If you must bring your phone, perhaps for safety, at least put it deep in your pocket and enjoy your surroundings! I recall noticing a large hole under an uprooted tree and standing there for a while imagining what species of animal might be living there and raising a family.

Seeing the positive in all around me is amazing and enlightening. If you find you are starting to give the negative mind more space in your brain, stop and switch to the lighter side. Similarly, working on defensiveness and judgements of others is a daily challenge for most of us. When I notice I am "doing it again", I endeavour to stop, listen to myself, and tell myself "enough of that" and look for the brighter side.'

I try to seek and look for the shiny side of an object, even though at times it is difficult to find. My dad would call it looking for the silver lining.

I will only get so much time on this earth. I want to enjoy it to the fullest. It simply does not make sense to waste my precious time on complaining about what isn't right, or what I don't like. My husband and I have lost a number of friends this year, some very suddenly. You just never know if you are to receive another day, another year, or another decade. Treating myself kindly every day is part of my solution to not fearing death. It is coming, whether I like it or not, so until that time, I want to "take it all in."

My friend in Vancouver said to me once that we need to slow down and allow nature to teach us. Her suggestion is to be still and watch nature. Stillness, she said speaks in an amazing way. Watch the activity of the birds at your bird feeder, or while sitting on a park bench, watch the chipmunks scurrying around with purpose on their busy day. If you want to gain more wisdom, she told me: "Be still and use your senses to their full capacity."

The Thirteenth Stair: Trusting Your Instincts

Trust your instincts.
Don't wait.
The time will never be just right.
It is not for me to know right now.
I know the answer is out in the universe, so don't worry about it.
I will know when I am meant to know."

—Unknown

The word "intuition" comes from the Latin word *intueri*, which means to contemplate or to look inwards. I needed to learn to trust my intuition rather than relying on advice given by others, or making a rash decision without thought. Your intuition is that "feeling" that you get that guides you on a certain path. Some would call it a gut feeling, a hunch, or having a sixth sense. Listening to my intuition and trusting those thoughts have been difficult for me. Sometimes, I hear it, then quickly dismiss it, and go ahead anyway. In the past, it seems that I always felt that I needed to check-in with someone else to ensure I was on the right staircase.

Trusting is a challenge for me. In the past, I learned that when I did trust someone I was often let down. The more that happens, the less likely I am to trust a situation or a person's word. As time passed, I was trusting others less and less. Through constant repetition of telling myself this, I came to believe it. "You can only trust yourself and no one else."

We are all shaped by our life experiences. For example, I took wedding vows and trusted that they were sacred. They certainly were for me. I never cheated on my spouse. I never deceived my partner. I never stole or broke the law. So, when this happened on the other side of these relationships by my partners, it re-enforced in my mind not to trust again. I was reluctant to even date as I knew where that would get me!

Another example is that I worked for a particular company for twenty-six years at a job that I absolutely loved, and then I was suddenly fired. My manager told me that she simply didn't think we could work together (after working for two weeks with her). Very shortly after that, I was told that a colleague, who I considered a friend, had betrayed me with our new manager and had encouraged her to let me go. I was angry. The working "friend" avoided me entirely, and I heard from a number of people that she was feeling guilty for her words and actions. This was a "friend" that we socialized with, and she had been at my home a number of times. This was the most difficult part of losing my job: losing the people I thought were friends. Again, this was another example in my mind of why not to trust anyone, including my own instincts.

I once saw an interview chat between Oprah Winfrey and Maya Angelou, and the quote that fits this section of my writing is:

> *When people show you who they are—why don't you believe them the first time?*
> *Why does it take twenty-nine times for you to get it?*
>
> —Maya Angelou

I knew my current husband for many years before we were a couple. I saw him married to my dear friend, and the marvellous way he treated her until she left this world. During our last conversation together in palliative care, I told her she was blessed to have such a caring and loving gentleman her whole life. She agreed 100%, and said she certainly couldn't have asked for a kinder partner. She joked that I should know, though, that he does have his faults! Still, when he asked me out some time later, I was hesitant (to ever get into a loving relationship again), but my instinct said this time it was right.

After leaving the job I was speaking of earlier, I went to work for a small architectural firm. I was cautious about building relationships, but as time went on, I really felt that I was making a difference within the firm and with the people who worked there. I realized that having trusting relationships and incredible job satisfaction was possible. It is rare in my experience, but possible.

Around the two-year mark of my journey, I heard a statement that stuck with me, and I wrote it in my journal: *"When you are on a path to being set free, you have to become less interested in what others think of us, and more interested in the whispers of your soul."* In other words, trust your intuition. After all, what others think of me is none of my business.

This notation in my journal resonated as I started to explore my lack of trust in others. I was realizing that I was focusing too much on what others were saying. I was subconsciously assuming that they must be right, and I must be wrong, so I took the words of others to heart. I saw that I was not listening to what I thought because I needed some sort of validation.

Deep down, I knew that I didn't believe in myself and was not loving myself. I was proud of my accomplishments in the work world, but I knew in my heart that I didn't believe that I was as worthy as those around me. Even thinking about my past failed marriages, I was still holding onto the false belief that they left because I did something wrong. I was not a good wife. I was not dedicated enough, attractive enough, smart enough. This is simply not true.

I wanted to start trusting my own truth. Others may have experiences in their lives that leads to their opinions and thoughts. However, I also have opinions, and I needed to learn to trust the wisdom I had acquired so far in my life.

I started re-reading my journals and saw the theme of not believing I was worthy over and over again. I was determined to re-set the start button and focus on this key point.

For example, when my recovery friends were starting to not show up to our Just for Today Zoom calls, and I was there, I took it personally. Of course, it wasn't logical that they wouldn't show up at the meeting to hurt ME. I had to constantly remind myself that it had nothing to do with me. It was possible that they were busy. It was possible they slept in. It was possible they relapsed. It was possible an emergency came up—or any of other infinite possibilities. I had to constantly remind myself that this had nothing to do with me. My focus needed to be redirected and not spending time on other people's business.

As I mentioned earlier, a counsellor at the treatment centre advised me to not let others take up valuable parking space in my brain. Your brain only holds so much at a time, and her point was not to waste those precious brain cells on something that you are making up in your mind (i.e., your negative assumptions).

Today, my mind still goes to playing the victim at times, but I am gradually learning to arrest that nonsense before it really blows up. Just taking a few moments to consider the other possibilities to my assumption takes practice, and it is still a work in progress for me.

Victim mode is that place you go in your mind when something did not go as you assumed or wanted it to go. For example: Let's say there was a party down the street and you were not invited. Victim mode is automatically assuming that it was intentional not to have you attend. But perhaps it was a mistake, perhaps it was for family only, perhaps your invite is in the mail and got lost. A couple of years ago I received two—not one, but two—Christmas cards in the mail in June of the following year. I don't know where they were all that time, but one was from someone locally that we see regularly, and the other was from an old school friend who lives in Ontario. My point is: Stuff happens!

When I realize that I am making a negative assumption, I try to look at the other side right away. For me, this is sort of making a pros and cons list when trying to make a decision. Depending on the importance of the situation, it may gnaw at me throughout the day, in which case, back to the beginning of stopping and considering the alternatives and letting it go.

Another example comes to mind on a broader level. Recently, someone said to me that they never give any money to a homeless person on the street because they "always" spend it on drugs or alcohol. How someone who is not homeless, and has abundance in their own lives, would know this as a fact is beyond me, but....

The old me would not say anything in response. The old and new me does frequently give to homeless people. The new me says that you can't make the assumption that all homeless are spending money on drugs and alcohol. Even if they are, they have a disease that has gotten out of hand, and who am I to judge that?

There are many, many reasons why someone may be living on the streets. I chose to help and to count my blessings that my life turned out differently, and that I have the resources to assist another human being. After all, we all started out the same, being born and lying in that little bassinet in the hospital nursery with a whole lifetime ahead of us. Some of us got a good start in life, and others did not.

Through my yoga practice and my incredible teacher, I started to be more focused on the actual words and mantras of my daily meditation. This sometimes means listening intentionally to the actual words of the music. I have acquired a small "library" of meditations that I participate in and repeat regularly. Some are focused on self-esteem, believing in yourself, dreaming of your full potential, or simply self-care. Others focus on the letting go of childhood negative memories or letting go of past hurts in general. After each practice, I journal about my learnings. I would read and re-read the positive statements. It reminded me of the saying I heard at rehab many times, "Fake it until you make it."

I no longer have anything to hide. If someone wants to judge me for my past mistakes, that is their business. I know I have made mistakes, and I am taking responsibility for them by living my life more truthfully and mindfully. I am human and will continue to make errors, and so will you. I have let go of continuing to chastise myself for those mistakes. There is nothing I can do about them, so I am moving on. I am no longer focusing on waiting for someone else to make amends to me. It is unlikely to happen, so I am not using my energy on it any more.

So back to intuition. Learning to trust myself and listening to my own thoughts, dreams, and opinions have afforded me the luxury of truly hearing myself. I mull them over and make a decision that is right for me. It may not be right for you, and you may disagree, and that is okay.

In striving for perfection and approval, I tried my best to avoid the discomfort of making mistakes. However, what I know now is if I don't make mistakes, I won't learn from the mistakes, and my life would be dull and stagnant. I want more joy, so I want to risk being wrong and screwing up and live more joyously by doing so! I want to dance through the rest of my life, not drag my feet through to the end. There is a Buddha saying I love: *"Each morning we are born again. What we do today is what matters."*

If I am unsure about something, but my intuition says it is right, then I tell myself to trust the process. In the past, if my intuition told me something (like, let's say, "Don't walk down the aisle, this marriage is not right for you…"), I would ignore it and justify the decision. After all, the guests are already here, and what would they say about my backing out? How would they treat me? How would they judge me? I recall cheering on Julia Roberts in *The Runaway Bride*, saying, "Good for you, girl!!!" Judged or not, she was listening to her own heart.

I recall a course I took many years ago, in which one of the teachings was, "What am I pretending not to know?" I have made it a practice to ask myself this question when sorting out a dilemma for myself. If the answer is "nothing", and I am being brutally honest with myself, then the decision becomes easier. It is interesting to me that it is easy to answer this question about *someone* in my life, but much more difficult to answer the question about *me*.

I have discovered that I am more joyful in my life from not pretending anymore. That feels amazing!

What is even more amazing is that the more successful I am at practicing my lessons, the more amazing it feels!

> *"You can't stop the waves, but you can learn to surf."*
> —Jon Kabat-Zinn, Author

The Fourteenth Stair: Tripping on a Stair

*In the midst of movement and chaos,
keep stillness inside of you.*

—Deepak Chopra

As we all have discovered, many times in our lives things don't always go as planned, and hence, we trip!

To be clear, I did not break my sobriety, but I sure thought about it. I decided to take the Mastermind course with Meg, my Kundalini teacher/coach. The events leading up to this decision were mind-blowing.

For a couple of years, I have been "told" on numerous occasions that my soul's purpose at this point in my life is to tell my story: my journey through my addiction and where I am at today in a place of joy. It started with the photograph of the quote from Brené Brown, which you read at the start of this book that said: *"One day you will tell your story of how you overcame what you went through, and it will be someone else's survival guide."* It was on my bulletin board for a couple of years, and I had basically forgotten about it. My focus at that time, returning from the treatment centre, was obviously sobriety. My focus was not writing a how-to guide as Ms. Brown suggests.

A friend from recovery said to me one day that she saw me as a wise soul, and that she appreciated and cherished my wisdom, my kind words and encouragement, and my positive outlook on the journey we were both on. I remember being on a recovery call when she said this, and my eyes were drawn to the photograph on my bulletin board. Perhaps the universe was telling me something. However, as I was in early recovery, about year two, I again put the thoughts aside.

On top of that, I was starting to focus on living more mindfully and on giving back to the community. I was giving back in a few ways through sewing quilts, knitting hats, etc., but I was not giving back to the community of recovery. I planted the seed for myself, suggesting that I start watching for clues in the universe as to what that giving back would look and feel like. How could I give back to the community of people who perhaps were still suffering, as I had, and were turning to unhealthy choices to numb out?

In the fall of 2022, I was staying on Vancouver Island for a month, and got together, individually, with several treatment centre "graduates". During chats over lunch about our futures, one said to me, "You should write a book about your journey." I laughed, and I recall saying that it sounded like a good idea, but….. The But was all about my not feeling I had enough to offer. My language art skills were rusty, and who would want to read it anyway? There were numerous other I can't, I won't, I am not capable statements. As we chatted, however, I became aware that the response in my head was always, "Yeah, but…." I was reminded that I had read many self-help books over the past couple of years, all in pursuit of finding tools to maintain my new lifestyle. Some were written by experts in the field, but some were written by "ordinary people like me". My outward response to my friend was that I would think about that possibility. Again, I briefly thought of the photo of the Brené Brown quote that was on my bulletin board.

The following March, I was back on the Island visiting my dear friend Joanne. Joanne knew of a holistic healing place that would balance my chakras, which was interesting, and we were going to try it just to see what it was all about. Through my work on my Kundalini yoga practice, I had been learning and working on balancing both the mind and the body. I had learned about the chakras during my practice and thought this would be an interesting experience. Sure enough, it was awesome! Over the course of the two hours, the practitioner seemed to know where all my aches and pains were. The session was fascinating, and I was feeling such a sense of calm, which I could only attribute to the balancing. As I was leaving my appointment, I noticed that another service offered by the healing centre was a psychic reading. I didn't have writing a book in the forefront of my mind at the time, but it sounded like fun to do the reading and see what came out of it.

A few days later, we were back at the healing centre where we each met individually with a woman named Ursula. Ursula is a published author of a spirituality book, and I immediately connected with her, in part because she and I have the same cultural heritage. I learned a lot in that hour about my complicated life. She specialized in seeing and talking to you about your past lives. She explained that understanding where our soul came from could be a very useful tool in our current life. Her belief was that our soul comes back in the future to "try again" to learn lessons, which we may not have gotten clarity on the first time we were on the planet. Whether you believe in this type of therapy or not, it is fascinating. As I have said before, we can always learn. and closing your eyes and ears to something different doesn't make it disappear. For me, it was new learning, and I was excited and curious.

During the session, I learned that I had lived at least twice on this planet, and she began to tell me about my experiences from long ago. Specifically, she zeroed in on two past lives many centuries ago that were fascinating and had a common thread to my current life. The common thread was that in both times that my soul was here on earth, I was regarded as a healer, and the people in my village, at each of these times, regarded me as a wise spiritual leader. She described people of my village coming to me for help with their problems. She described me as a nine-year-old Black girl with bright blue eyes in Africa in the 1500s. Because of the colour of my eyes, the villagers were a bit afraid of me, but knew I could assist them. In that life time I lived to be 111 years old, until I stated I was tired and wanted to move on from this earth.

The second life she saw me in was in the 1600s as an eleven- or twelve-year-old where I was living in a locked, small brick room as I was a healer, and people were afraid of me. My mother at the time kept me there as she feared that I would be harmed if I was out in the community. Pretty strange, but the second mention as a healer intrigued me.

Back to the present day, Ursula said that I was meant to share my journey with the people sitting on a steep staircase waiting to hear my wisdom. Whether you have a belief in this type of work or not, it was a bit unsettling for her to suggest this, as I certainly had heard this before. She went on to tell me to consider writing a book as the venue to share my story. She said I was meant to do this, and this was my soul's purpose. (She was not aware of the photo or the fact that I was in recovery.) As I left Ursula, she stopped me and told me that the aura around me was very bright. She also said that the shape of my aura also matched my body outline, which she said was very unusual.

These final comments from Ursula were intriguing, but not knowing anything about auras, I left it at that. Later that evening, Joanne and I were out to dinner with some of her friends, and one commented that I was "glowing". Was that the aura mentioned earlier in the day? I'm not sure, but it got me thinking.

The following day, during my regular meditation, I realized I was feeling unusually free, happy, and confident. My thoughts drifted to the words I had heard the day before, and I recalled another thing that Ursula said. She commented that there were three people in my life (two of whom were a couple) who were very intimidated by me, yet pretending to be in my court as friends (or family). She attributed this to my being on a higher level of spirituality, and therefore, these three people were not understanding me and being cautious around me. I don't know who these people are, but she had also said that it did not matter who they are. She reminded me not to take up space in my brain trying to figure out who it was, as it really didn't matter.

She said I was strong and needed to pursue the sharing of wisdom as discussed. "You were meant to help others in this world, and the way to do that could be the writing and distribution of a book." *Fascinating*, I thought. Was this the third sign from the universe—the photo being one, my recovery friend suggesting this, and now Ursula?

Two days later, I met with another friend, Jamie. She had gone to treatment about a year after me, but we were connected by another friend from recovery who said at the time that she felt we would connect with each other. Jamie and I have been Zooming ever since.

As a surprise for my birthday, Jamie arranged for me to talk to a psychic. What a beautiful gift! I was excited and very curious if the two readers would carry similar messages to me. There are many skeptics in this world on this sort of thing, but it is my belief that this is a gift that some are given, and their sharing of this gift is beautiful.

This reading was a bit more relatable to me, as she spoke more of the present and future than Ursula had. This reading blew my mind. She started with suggesting that I should be gentler with myself and less critical of my abilities. She said that I needed to step up into my confidence, and do the things I was meant to do. She spoke of being open to all possibilities coming up for me shortly. She went on to say that doors were opening for me that I would never have imagined before. She encouraged me to explore my spiritual nature, which is a large part of my being. She suggested I start a business, change would be coming my way, and that I would receive much help in this regard. She suggested that I consider looking into practicing Kundalini yoga! Little did she know that I had been practising this type of yoga for the last two and a half years.

Her next statement was powerful. "You will have the support you need to write a book that will help others." She suggested that I just start writing, and that process in itself would release any self-doubt. She also said that I should write about a recent journey, putting a personal perspective on its difficulties.

She was not at all aware of the recent signs I had received in terms of writing a book. She also was not made aware in advance that I was in recovery—a recovery that I call my journey. Nor did she know that I was already very involved with a Kundalini practice and that my teacher/mentor was about to announce some course work that would lend itself to pursuing this possibility.

My friend Jamie was with me during the reading and took notes for me. This would prove very valuable later, as some of the points made by the psychic seemed unlikely at the time. However, re-reading the notes after some time had passed revealed that more and more of her points were coming to fruition.

I felt amazing when I got home and overwhelmed with the knowledge I had gained while on the Island. Two days after arriving home, during my regular Kundalini practice, our teacher posed a question to the group: "How can you expand and move towards your deepest desire?"

Over the course of the next few weeks, I could not believe the number of subtle reminders from the universe that were whispering to me.

What the heck, I told myself, and I started to write and write and write. The words were flowing out of me like some sort of magical spell. I noticed small things around me and knew that somehow they were meant for me to listen to and act upon.

For example, on my one-thousandth day of recovery, the theme of that day's yoga practice was "to embrace my self-sourced power and to share my magic with the world." I had to wonder if that meant I should write a book or if it was referring to the book that the psychic on the island recommended to me, which was called *Big Magic* by Elizabeth Gilbert.

After practice, I was off to the bookstore. I purchased a copy of that book and started to absorb Elizabeth's magic! It has always been my belief that everything happens for a reason and comes to us when we need it.

> *Allow yourself to rest. Your soul speaks to you in the quiet moments in between your thoughts.*
>
> —Author Unknown

I knew in my heart that the universe was speaking to me, and that this whirlwind of thoughts and curious happenings were coming my way for a reason. During this time, I received a random email from a long-lost friend asking about re-connecting with each other.

I was glancing at my bookcase, noticed an old book, and I had the feeling I should pick it up and glance through it. It was a book I had bought some time earlier called *The Circle of Stones* by Judith Duerk. I took it off the shelf to re-read.

Re-reading this powerful book, I had this sense that the universe was telling me something. I had also dreamed about my dad a couple of times and was feeling his encouragement from the other side. All of this seemed to be telling me that I was meant to embark on a powerful journey.

All of this back story led me to the calling I felt to connect with Meghan, my teacher/coach about her course I mentioned earlier. I read, and re-read, the material promoting the Mastermind course called Chrysalis, she was about to start, all the while switching back and forth from "this is not for me, it is for other humans" to "this was meant to come to me at this time and place."

I had an overwhelming feeling that this course would be THE jewel in my crown of pursuing my dream. Up until this point, the book was an idea, but now I was seeing it and calling it a dream that I was meant to fulfill. It was a lot of money for the course by my standards, and the doubt of my not being worthy enough to spend that kind of money on ME slipped in and out of my head.

Finally, I made the call and signed up. After all, I had been on a journey that, in part, was about being more mindful and living in the moment. *What am I waiting for?* I asked myself. *Take the leap into the unknown, Cheryl.*

About week two of the mastermind course, I felt like I was drowning. I had been out of the workforce at this point for over seven years. The small group taking the course was very diverse. A few had businesses already, one had written several books, others were just starting out looking for magic in their lives. The first session was exciting. The following day, in pursuit of working on the assignments, I realized that my technical online knowledge was right back in the Dark Ages. It had been years since I had to learn a new computer skill, and when I was in the workforce, there had been an IT department down the hallway if I got stuck.

After hours of tackling how to download and use all these new programs and tools, I had a meltdown. I was questioning myself on what I had gotten into and if I was cut out for it. I was full on doubting myself and my capabilities. Here I was seventy-two hours in and thinking about giving up? The tears had never flowed so quickly and in such volume since being in treatment. I was afraid that I was once again on the slippery slope of negativity and hopelessness. The following day, I had a 1:1 call with my teacher that really helped get me back on track. That and Roger by my side with his tremendous support and encouragement worked wonders.

I was relieved that breaking my sobriety had not come into play, but I was also very consciously aware that it could have easily come into play. I was determined to stay on course with that aspect of my life. I was also overcome with gratitude for those around me who were supporting me in my endeavour.

What I learned from that day was to slow down and take my time. There is no rush where creativity is concerned. Also, I reminded myself to stop beating myself up with negative talk about all the things I could not do, or learn to do. I knew that I needed to walk away and take some quiet time to re-group. I went for a walk, breathed in the air, and talked to myself about gratitude. Once I calmed down with deep breathing and (quite honestly) stopped crying, I knew that doing a meditation would be effective. But in the moment, I was panicked, and it took my dear partner to remind me of the tools I had in the toolbox. I knew I had this huge toolbox of strategies, but sometimes as a mere mortal, I need to be reminded. I know that this is okay.

As you know by now, part of my daily routine is to read the quote of the day from my daily mindfulness book and reflect on it during my meditation. On this particular day the quote was:

> *I can't change the directions of the wind, but I can adjust my sails to always reach my destination.*
>
> —Jimmy Dean

Okay, I am determined to honour that one! I wrote in bold, coloured letters in my journal: *Are you in or are you out, Cheryl?*

I tell you this story to remind you, and to remind myself, that life is full of challenges and hard times, but also great expansive experiences. Taking a risk can be invigorating.

The Fifteenth Stair: The Art of Journaling (According to Me!)

Journaling is like whispering to one's self and listening at the same time.

—Mina Murray, *Dracula*

believe that each and every one of us is living a journey of our own. We can all be teachers and healers in some form, as what we have to say counts. I have learned that being a teacher or a healer does not necessarily mean teaching and healing others. For me, my teacher comes from within and is teaching me, and when I learn the lessons, that is healing.

I see my journal as my unconditional friend and companion. I can tell "her" my inner most thoughts, dreams, and fears without receiving any judgement. She never complains to me. She is one of my teachers, perhaps my most valuable.

I like to communicate with my journal every day. It does not matter what is written in this special book. It only matters that it contains my innermost thoughts: thoughts that are difficult and/ or joyous. A journal is private, and you can express yourself in the bluntest of ways. The more honest you are in your writings, the better. I see my journal as a place to express myself in raw honesty. If you were to read some of my journal pages during difficult times, you might get the impression that I was ready to throw in the towel on life. No, I am simply just getting it all out in the open and expressing my feelings.

Sometimes what is said in my journal is not pretty. I don't worry about being messy, or about spelling or grammar. I am no artist in terms of drawing or painting but, occasionally, I do add in drawings or other visuals with my pencil crayons.

Look out for the book by Emily Carr called *Sister and I from Victoria to London*. It is a beautiful book that I purchased at the

Victoria Museum. It is a journal, handwritten by Ms. Carr, describing an adventure she and her sister Alice had over a hundred years ago. In between the words, written in 1910, are lovely watercolour paintings by Ms. Carr. Watercolour is not a medium usually associated with Ms. Carr's work, but the paintings are exquisite.

The forward of the book explains that the original journal was written using a standard exercise book on pages framed by borders of red lines. The question is: Are you old enough to remember those standard issue books? Perhaps you don't, but I do! I bring this point up as you don't need a fancy leather-bound journal (that potentially you are afraid to write in because it is so beautiful!).

Another book to look out for is called *Rooms of Their Own—Where Great Writers Write* by Alex Johnson with illustrations by James Oses. It is a beautiful book with watercolour paintings and two or three pages devoted to each writer from Margaret Atwood and Jane Austen to Virginia Woolf and Mark Twain. It talks about the where and how of their writing habits, their routines, and quirky habits and rituals. It also talks about the spaces where they got inspired: Maya Angelou found her best inspirations in hotel rooms; Agatha Christie had her best writing ideas while washing dishes; and Hemingway got his inspiration in his bedroom, in which the walls were graced with stuffed heads from his hunting trips. Some only wrote during the night, some only during the day, some at home with a bustling family, and some only in seclusion. I would love to have the artistic talent to add watercolour paintings to my journal, but I don't. If you have that talent, go for it! So, from ink wells to pencils, special pens to typewriters and then to computers, the great ones had their unique ways of reaching us with their magical books. This book is an inspirational tabletop book, that I randomly open to a new discovery.

Getting Started

Visit your local bookstore. I personally love Indigo for this type of purchase. They have a wide selection of not only blank journals, but also journals that have journal prompts to get you started. You will find that journals range from leather bound, vegan leather bound, or paper. Some are pretty, and perhaps have a drawing on the front that speaks to you. Some have initials on them, making them just for you, the writer. Alternately go to the dollar store and find something there. I find it easiest to write in a book that lies fairly flat when open. It really doesn't matter which you choose. For me I like a pretty one! Choose what speaks to you.

While at the book or stationary store, select a writing instrument that brings you love. A pen that is just for journaling vs. the promotional pen in the back of your junk drawer. My tools for journaling are specially hand selected by me, for me. Does that sound a bit silly ? Perhaps, but it brings me joy and makes my writing feel special! It feels the same as when you feel spectacular when you are all dressed up to go out on the town. That is how I see my journaling tools.

Start Writing

The front of each of my journals are signed, and dated with a start date. After a book is full, I return to the front and put in an end date before it finds its home on my bookshelf. I date each entry as a reference point, and I know some people who also include the weather temperature for the day. Not my thing, but make your journal uniquely yours.

You can write about anything; perhaps something you saw in nature on a walk. For example, today I sat on a bench in the park during my walk and watched a family of mallard ducks tend to their new ducklings. It was fascinating how calmly those parents worked with their new off-spring. The little ones were falling all over themselves, learning to walk. The fathers were over to the side watching, and the mama was tending to the ducklings, chirping at them occasionally. I assume that ducks have their own language, but don't know that for sure! The calm of their interactions inspired me, and I wrote not only about this scene, but also about creating more calm in my life.

I often refer to my daily Mindfulness book that I have mentioned a few times, and I will often record the quote of the day and then write about what that quote means to me at that moment in time. For instance, the quote in my book today as I write this page says: "Feelings are just visitors, let them come and go." (Mooji)

Recently, I was quite anxious over the course of a couple of days regarding a project I was working on, and therefore I wrote about those feelings. I wrote and wrote until the anxiousness started to subside. I do that, as I remember hearing from someone that if you keep telling the story that is weighing on your mind over and over—keep talking (or in this case writing) about what is consuming your mind—that it will eventually start to lose its power so you gain clarity.

Another way of starting your writing for the day is to list an item or two that you are grateful for. For example, today I am grateful for the much-needed rain outside; I am grateful for my husband listening to me last evening by lending me his ear as I spoke of the challenges I was facing about my project; I am grateful for the roof over my head as I watch the news depicting the devastation of all of the wild fires this year; I am grateful for the freedom I have to sit in my writing room, sipping my tea and writing these words.

I know someone who starts each entry with a few phrases of prayer. Her faith is sacred to her, and therefore, this personally speaks to her.

Another friend reserves her journal for hopes, dreams, goals, and bucket list items. Whatever you write is up to you, as it is yours, and no one else's. Whatever comes to you. There is no judgement here. It is your sacred book and companion.

At this stage in my recovery journey, I mostly write about my activities and thoughts around what I am doing to stay clean and mindful. I like listening to podcasts and often will jot down a thought I have heard there, and then write to contemplate it further.

Consider incorporating into your journal some drawings, scribblings, stickers … whatever makes you happy. Paint as if you are Emily Carr. Perhaps, you truly are a painter, and in that case, go for it!

Why Journal?

Everyone who takes the time to write in a journal does it for a different reason. I want to share with you my biggest reason for faithfully writing daily. It is to re-read them and learn from the past. I often read about how I dealt with a similar situation to one I find myself in now. This allows me to see how I emotionally reacted to a given event back then as opposed to the newer, wiser person I feel I am becoming. Let me give you an example. In researching this book, I re-read my collection of journals. I discovered how far I had come in the last three-plus years by reading about my reaction to someone judging me in the past. The anger and resentment I felt back then affected the rest of my day/week. Reflecting on how I react today to a similar situation gives me strength to carry on, as I see progress, I hear progress, and I feel progress.

Re-reading that part of my journey reminds me I am working on being a better me, and that inspires me to continue. It gives me courage to push myself forward a bit more every day. All of that makes me proud and full of Joy.

I find re-reading my old journals helpful towards my growth. I can see from the first entry while on my way to the treatment centre how frightened and anxious I was. I find it helps me now when I am frightened about an upcoming event or situation to compare and see that time truly does heal, and therefore, this present challenge will eventually fade as well.

If you are considering utilizing this healing tool, try to do it daily for a few months without fail. Re-read, see what you see, learn what you learn, and hear what you hear. Only then can you make an informed choice if this is a tool for your own toolbox.

So long as you write what you wish to write,
that is all that matters; and whether it
matters for ages or only for hours, nobody can say.

—Virginia Woolf (1882–1941)

According to *Rooms of Their Own*, the book I was speaking about earlier in this chapter, Virginia wrote in an old writing shed located under a chestnut tree in her garden in East Sussex. The windows were rattled at one point by Nazi bombs. She loved to write on blue writing paper, and her friend once wrote that she was always surrounded by filth packets ... old pen nibs, bits of paper, and cigarette ends!

The Sixteenth Stair: Food for Thought

*Life isn't about getting and having,
it's about giving and being.*

—Kevin Kruse, Historian and Professor at Princeton

The following "Food for Thought" may be used as journal prompts, or you can just read through them and consider how they apply to your current life. These are a bit of a summation of what I have come to realize and have learned over these three-plus years.

Age Is Only a Number

I thought before this particular journey that I was too old to start something new. I wasn't too old for sobriety, of course, but write a book? I figured that I am retired, and therefore "work" is over, and now life is about leisure only. There is only so much travelling you can do, and after a while, you may become sickened of that as well. Some time ago, I was participating in a conversation about retirement, and the talk turned to a couple who had sold their home and bought a fancy-dance motor home. Their intention in retirement was to drive everywhere on the continent. After eighteen months or so, they were longing for the comfort of "home" with their family and friends. They hadn't considered that not seeing those in their circle would be missed as much as it was. They loved the adventure they took during that timeframe, and all the new experiences and people, but they knew they wanted to settle back into their nest.

That got me thinking about some recent stories in the news in 2023 about people doing things that were out of the norm age-wise. Consider Rut Linnea Ingegard Larsson from Sweden, who went skydiving in May 2022 and broke the Guinness World Record for the oldest skydiver. Her first dive was at the young age of ninety, but she broke this record a bit later at age 103!

Think about "Hurricane Hazel": Hazel McCallion was the mayor of Mississauga, Ontario for thirty-six years until her retirement in 2014. She was certainly a fire-cracker in her time. She was 101 when she passed in early 2023.

The other day, the local news featured a ninety-two-year-old woman who had regularly written stories and thoughts in her journals (for decades) and was encouraged to put them together in a book. She said she dismissed the idea at first but was convinced to go ahead. She had ordered one hundred copies of the book from the publisher, thinking that there would be way too many left over. Almost immediately, the publisher could not keep up with the orders for a copy of it. What a delightful interview this was on the news, and I was inspired for sure, squashing the idea that I was too old to write what you are reading now!

And, what about Fauna Singh in Toronto, who in June of 2023 ran a marathon? He was one hundred years young.

Then there is my husband who recently hit the eight-decade mark. He had always wanted to learn to play an instrument, and sure enough, that Christmas I bought him a ukulele and some lessons at the shop. He loves it!

The lesson here is that age has nothing to do with whether or not you can start a new chapter on something you have always wanted to accomplish. Age is only a number.

Achieving Longevity

There is a regular study in the world that is conducted by Global Health, which looks at the top countries for longevity and health, called the "blue zones". People who live in a blue zone, experience lower rates of cancer, heart disease, and other non-communicable diseases associated with age and lifestyle. People living in the blue zones have more centurions living than other places in the world. The blue zones come down to a variety of factors like low-stress lifestyles, plant-based diets, and belonging to communities (in many cases religious).

Here are the top four:

Sardinia, Italy: This blue zone is attributed to a low-stress lifestyle and a strong sense of community, which largely comes from faith, but also in supporting others—giving back and making sure all are well in the circle.

Okinawa, Japan: This is a small island south of Japan, and it is known for having more centurions in their country than any other place on the planet. Clean diet and daily exercise, including daily dance are two key elements. Again, there is a strong sense of community there, and this area is also rated near the top of the happiest people in the world.

Ikaria, Greece: This is an island that is referred to as "the place where people forget to die". Their secret is daily community socializing, which combats depression and loneliness as we age. An example is that every day, the citizens meet with their buddies over coffee or a chess game in the town square.

Nicoya, Costa Rica: The people here attribute their longevity to seeking and having "purpose" in their lives—whether it is work, faith, or hobbies. Everyone has a purpose and lives to fulfill that purpose.

In thinking about these centurions, I am becoming more aware of clean diets, which have no processed foods, no added sugars, very little meat, and certainly no "junk food". Smoking, alcohol, and drugs are rare in these blue zones, and home remedies are passed from generation to generation. The other common denominator seems to be a strong sense of community.

This is an area that North Americans can certainly learn from, as it is not unusual here for families to be spread across the country instead of staying put for generations and learning from their elders. But most of all, what resonates with me is the slower pace; a pace that doesn't require all the should-do's or must-do's that we are often raised with or learn over time.

Happiest Cultures/Countries

For six years running, Finland is the happiest country in the world, followed by Denmark, Iceland, Israel, and the Netherlands (2023). What are they doing that we can replicate?

High satisfaction with their relationships is key. This would include services that the government looks after such as shorter workweeks, equality in education, free higher education, and national pension and health care plans so that people don't have to worry about these and can focus on other areas of their lives. Generous family leaves and free daycare are also provided. This creates a society with very low poverty and crime rates, which contribute to some of the happiness factors. Yes, their taxes are higher, but because of the basic needs covered, people are able to focus on their lives and what brings them joy.

In watching several documentaries gathering this information, people allow their children to play outside with friends and are able to walk the streets with no anxiousness about "something" happening to them at the hands of others.

I learned that, yes, they have people immigrating to their country from different parts of the globe, but they say that happiness is contagious, and foreigners quickly adapt to the culture. Finland also has the cleanest water in the world.

What have I learned here? I wanted to understand what makes the people in the Nordic countries so happy, take ideas out of that, and apply it to my life. Of course, I can't do anything about what our Canadian government supplies or doesn't supply for us. I was searching out other factors I could incorporate into my life—and that you could incorporate into your life.

Reading more about the relationships that people in Denmark have, it seems friendships and families are at the top of the list. This gets me thinking about connections and ensuring that I expand my community and reach out, particularly to those in need. Also, these countries give considerably more paid vacation time than in North America, to relax and rejuvenate their peoples' bodies and souls. This would suggest to me that, regardless of how busy your life is, taking time to relax is key to your overall happiness. I believe that we should make this a priority in life.

Danish people say, "You go first; take care of yourself first." Fun fact: More than half the population has a large sauna at their home or business. The rule of the sauna is that there is no arguing inside. So when business people are negotiating business, their discussion with a client sometimes takes place in a sauna as it will be a productive discussion without arguing. The same practice is incorporated into family life.

People Come and Go

Author and Artist, Flavia Weedn said: *Some people come into our lives and leave footprints on our hearts, and we are never the same.* We meet new people almost every day, that is, if we are taking the time to say hello and to listen to their views.

I used to feel I was often abandoned by those who came into my life and then disappeared. (I think a younger generation calls it "being ghosted".) I still at times have that sense, but I am learning that sometimes people are meant to come into your life at a particular time and not necessarily continue to be in your circle. Perhaps the universe connected you with someone you were meant to learn from.

Not everyone we meet will be a lifelong friend ,and that is simply okay. An example could be when you had a good friend in early life that you no longer keep in contact with. Your lives changed. Perhaps you had a demanding career with lots of travel, and now your friend is happily settled in suburbia with their five children. There was not a falling out necessarily; you just followed different paths.

Taking the time to engage in conversation with someone not in your "normal" circle is life changing.

I find, that:

- I may learn something I never knew.
- The other person may learn something new from me.
- I have the opportunity to expand my mind and consider something I never thought of.
- They may point me in a different direction than I was thinking when I was grappling with a decision.
- The person may become a long-term friend.

Having people around me with different views is not only healthy, but expands my mind about the world. The opposite would be staying in the same box/house/neighbourhood, etc., and seeing the world in only one way. For example, if the only ones you discuss the news with are people who agree with you, it reinforces that view. That view may be one-sided, and so the circle of conversation is the same old same old. If it is a controversial or negative subject matter, then the negativity continues to feed itself. And, I would say that negativity has a huge appetite!

I will never forget my conversations with Sam, the man I met who wanted to see the world without cloudy eyes that I wrote about earlier in this book. What an impact it made for me to talk to someone whose upbringing could not have been more polar opposite than my experience. The lessons I learned from him will not quickly be forgotten.

When I was in treatment, I also got to know a gentleman from Inuvik. We had a number of interesting conversations, including about food. For him, the food at the centre was totally foreign, as he was used to eating—among other items—fresh, raw seal rather than overcooked chicken. He was also used to eating raw Arctic Char, a favourite. Word got around, and the chef brought in Arctic Char for him as a special treat.

I sat with him at dinner that evening and asked about his meal. He chuckled and said it was okay; the thought was wonderful, but the chef had cooked it. Good intentions gone sideways.

In another conversation with him as I was trying to learn about his culture, he said to me, "You southern people (anyone south of the North Pole) call us Eskimos, but we in our culture do not use that term." He went on to explain that it was a White man's term, and that it was considered by his people to be as derogatory as calling a Black man the "n" word. A couple of years ago when my city's football team was changing its name from the Eskimos to the Elks, I smiled and thought of my conversations with this man. Interesting what you learn.

Decades ago, when I was travelling quite a lot for my job, I was sitting next to a woman about my age on an airplane, and we got to talking about why we were travelling. She was going to a place in California to participate in a painting artists' retreat. She said that her son had now left home, and she always wanted to learn to paint. She had heard of this isolated place for like-minded women to learn the skills over a month-long period. I recall over the flight being so impressed with this human for leaping into her dream and travelling quite far to pursue this. I took down the information, but at the time, I put it aside. Sometimes I think of her and wonder how that all turned out, and I also wish I still had the contact info for the retreat!

Stop Blaming

I have learned that when I stop blaming someone else or an organization for what is happening in *my* life that I don't like or want, I am much happier. Letting go of resentments can be a life-changer in my mind. I found some of the feelings I was harbouring were blown out of proportion over the years, yet were still affecting me daily.

Finally letting go of that old story from childhood or your younger years can allow you to focus on happier things. I spent a lot of unnecessary time blaming others and the company I worked for after losing my job. All it did was heighten the anger. When that was finally dealt with, I was able to look back to the memorable moments of that job that I loved and cherished. The same could go for difficult relationships in my life. When I finally let that anger go, I could look back and learn the lessons I was meant to learn. That is not to say that the relationships are necessarily repaired, and we are "all good now". Not at all; it simply means that I am no longer giving those stories fuel or allowing them to consume my energy.

Not only does it not make sense to spend your energy on this for the sake of your mental health, but holding on to resentments also shows up in our bodies as aches, pain, disease, sluggishness, etc. For example, when you are anxious about an event or an interaction with someone, do you feel it in the pit of your stomach? Does it manifest itself into a raging headache? Does it affect your sleeping patterns? As my mentor/teacher says, listen to your body, and pay attention. Part of my reason for practicing Kundalini yoga is to learn to release past trauma or hurts from my physical body.

Along that same line, there is not always someone to blame, and the resentment builds up anyway. For example, why do some of the nicest people get a life-threatening disease and others do not? Other than the obvious factors that are known to cause certain health issues, why did that healthy person who eats right and exercises regularly get a tumour and a shortened time left on earth? I have learned that taking care of yourself will certainly contribute to your life, but there are no guarantees.

Use Caution Around Assumptions

I discovered for myself that I was quite quick to make a judgement, which included assumptions in the back of my mind. For example, you haven't called me for months, so I assume I did something wrong and that you are backing out of a relationship with me. Your thank-you note (if you sent one!) is late, so I assume that you didn't like the gift.

I can recall so many ridiculous examples like these. My life lesson was that I was filling up bags and bags of these assumptions, and then I wondered why I was a bit anti-social and resorted to my addiction to "help"?

I learned to not jump to conclusions. If I do feel I was wronged, I try to watch for more evidence with a clear mind, so I can make a proper decision. If there is more evidence, well at least it was thought through this time.

The Seventeenth Stair: Secret Medicines & Miracles

There are two ways to live your life.
One is as though nothing is a miracle.
The other is as though everything is a miracle.

—Albert Einstein

It has become more and more clear, as time goes on, that worrying about things doesn't take away tomorrow's troubles; it takes away today's peace. Live today. Yesterday is already gone. Who knows what tomorrow will bring?

Therefore, I starting to think about my secret medicines. Do you have secret medicines? For me, these are the activities in my life that bring me much peace and happiness. Consider something you do that when completed, you think to yourself: "Ahhh, what a wonderful day I had today." What makes you feel that: "I am inspired to continue on this journey?" What makes you say: "I will persevere and continue seeking?"

Meditation

As I was starting year three, I was considering what my medicines were. My first go-to medicine is doing a yoga practice and/or a meditation. Over the course of this journey, I have many meditations at my fingertips and certainly have some favourites. I particularly love ones that entail deep breathing and visualizing a future event or feeling. There is something about the rhythm of a meditation that brings total calm to me. On those days that are rushed, and I skip this, I feel it adversely in my body and mind.

Back when I was working full time, I recall a past mentor telling me that you get what you focus on. Therefore, I focus on a future event that I am hoping for and allow my mind to wander where it would like around that event.

During a class I was taking, this mentor gave the group a homework assignment. She asked us who had read the newspaper that morning. Most had. She asked if there were any advertisements for refrigerators in the paper. No one in the room had noticed. Then she suggested that if one of us was thinking of buying a refrigerator, the ads for this item would pop out at us, because in the back of our mind, we are aware we are looking for a fridge.

She also asked us how many red cars we had seen on our commute that morning. Again, no one had a true answer. Unknown to us, she had planted a seed, because at the start of the second day, she once again asked how many red cars were on our commute. Most of the small group had remembered that, perhaps in our unconscious mind, and had counted them that morning.

During my meditation this morning, I saw a little cabin surrounded by nature and heard all of its sounds. I could see the magnificent trees and the forest floor covered in green fauna. Occasionally, I would see little creatures flitting about, chatting with each other. I am sipping a hibiscus herbal tea out of my favourite pottery mug while writing my thoughts and reflections. The tea is steaming hot, and the added touch of fresh mint leaves from my garden makes it so aromatic.

The cabin is near the ocean, and I can hear the crashing waves against the shore. I picture the waves coming at me with new thoughts, new life, new ways of approaching my challenges, and the waves flowing back out to sea are taking away the negative, the regrets, the past hurts and events. I also hear the sounds of hundreds of birds chirping and going about their busy lives. Perhaps they are making a new nest for their family, teaching their little ones to fly, or just chatting about life! Then a couple of months later, we were on the Island again, and we took daily walks in Beacon Hill Park in Victoria, minutes from the ocean. The ocean and nature are a couple of my medicines.

We all feel at times that there are not enough hours in the day, and it is easy to resist a part of your new approach to your life. My life also gets hectic, so at times when I feel there is no time to do a formal meditation or healing practice, I will do one that is less structured. I can be sitting in a waiting room or on my deck and simply close my eyes and slow my thoughts. I have stopped listening to the radio in my car these days. I prefer putting the soft piano CD in and humming to it as I drive. It may mean consciously doing some deep breathing and listening to what I am hearing.

Sometimes what I hear is my own inner thoughts. Other times, I am listening to my surroundings: the sound of a car, the sound of a bird, the sound of children playing in the neighbours' yard. I try to make sure I am not simultaneously making a grocery list or planning what I am making for dinner today. It takes practice to be still, so if you find yourself drifting, just stop, take a deep breath, and re-focus. It does take conscious practice, and it will come over time. I wrote in a journal at some point: "Look at the beauty of the world as it is the first step of clearing your mind." It will take time, but persevere as it is worth the time. Don't give up, it will come. I am getting better at remaining on target, but some days I still have "monkey brain".

Learning

My next medicine is learning. This takes a few forms for me. I love to read, and in particular, reading a book from which I am learning something new. I admit that I am a collector of "paper books" as I generally read a non-fiction book with a highlighter in my hand, marking my learnings for review at another time. I will very often pick up that book again in the future, and if nothing else, re-read the highlights to remind me of the wisdom I gathered the first time I read it.

To supplement the book, I also seek out the author online and look for a podcast to hear their voice, which will often cement the learnings in my mind, as I picture myself in a real conversation with the author. Listening to a powerful podcast excites me. I can hear the energy in the author's voice and find myself saying, "I want more!" No matter what, I always take notes for future reference. Personally, I find it grounds the learnings in my brain when I use another sense besides reading.

I find that when I am reading, I learn. When I re-read it out loud, I really get it. I love when I am alone and can read a book out loud with feeling! It feels empowering to me, and I hear the message of the author more clearly. Confession here: If alone, I often can be found walking around the house reading a book out loud. Hint: It helps getting your steps in too!

If it is a fictional book, then I try to immerse myself in the book, picturing the surroundings as if I was living right there in the story. I enjoy analyzing the characters and trying to understand their thought process and their hopes and dreams, and reflecting on the book's ending. In particular, I love historical fiction for deepening my understanding of different times, cultures, and norms of that era. I love imagining what it would have been like with the challenges of those ancient times.

There is a website called "The Daily Om", which I subscribed to for free. It comes to my mail daily. It is usually a page or two article on a different aspect of living a fuller life. These daily articles can inspire you to look into a subject matter more fully. You can also subscribe to receive a daily horoscope if that is part of your interests. All of these offerings are free of charge.

Another area of the Daily Om is to sign up for one of the over 350 courses offered for a very small price tag. Some courses are designed for a daily lesson over the course of a week, or a weekly lesson over the course of several months. There are ones that will last for even longer. I have taken many of these affordable courses. One example was a basic yoga course that I took over the course of six weeks. After taking a course, you have it for life. The lessons don't expire! Therefore, you can take a refresher as needed!

Subjects are organized in categories such as: Health and Wellness; Self Development; Creativity; Family and other Relationships; Money and Career; Meditation; Spirituality, and many more. Each course offers an outline and bio of the instructor and suggested prices. Usually there are three prices offered, and you choose what you can afford. As I recall, the basic yoga course that I took some time ago was $35 for the six weeks. I have found all that I have enrolled in very worthwhile. So, check it out at: www.dailyom.com. Learning, as I said, is a medicine for me, and medicine is wonderful for bringing more joy into my life. Perhaps it will do the same for you.

My learning medicine inspires me to do greater things. It inspires me to reach higher and higher for more knowledge. My life is no longer a series of events or experiences that I trudge through day after day. Now, my life is about learning, growing, and seeking more wisdom and joy.

Creating

Another medicine for me is quilting. There is something very calming for me in cutting out dozens and dozens of tiny pieces of fabric and stitching them together into a cozy reading blanket or quilt. As I said earlier, I also find great joy in creating a quilt for a friend or to give to a charity, knowing that someone in the universe has a cozy piece of a love blanket. I made one a few years back for a silent auction for breast cancer, which raised over $500. I have friends who love other creative activities such as scrapbooking, knitting, playing a musical instrument, restoring an old car, painting, etc. Activities like these take me away from my busy mind and into a place of calm and satisfaction.

Is there an activity that you used to do before you fell into a mundane existence or before your addiction took over your life? Maybe there is a childhood memory of loving to draw or colour as a child. Maybe it is the time to resurrect that past time.

I remember in my early teens that my dad was in the hospital. He had been sick for some time, and the medical world was puzzled by his symptoms. Somewhere along the line, my mom mentioned to the doctors about a dark mole on his back that once in a while was oozing. Checking into it, my dad had some sort of bite from an unknown bug that had made its way to his stomach and was basically eating all of the nutrition out of his body.

Dad travelled regularly to Africa on business, and it was assumed it was from one of his trips. He was admitted to what they then called "the foreign disease" ward of the hospital and was in isolation. I remember visiting him in the hospital and talking to him through a window.

In any case, Dad, who was used to working as an engineer, was quite frankly bored during that hospital isolation. I recall him asking for drawing materials—perhaps some paper and charcoals. During the course of the next few weeks (four to five, as I recall) he started drawing and discovered that he was quite talented. This hobby was something he had not done for years and was re-discovering it and the talent he had for it.

In later years, when he retired, Dad expanded on this talent, took lessons, and started painting. The point of this story is that this was medicine for my dad. He picked up on something he recalled from his past and starting exploring it again. As I write this story, his painting of his original homestead is on the wall above me.

Other Medicines

As I embarked on this writing project, I started asking others what their medicines were. My husband loves to cycle—not competitively, but for pleasure. He recently bought an e-bike, and his favourite place to ride is in the parks and trails in our river valley. He loves the quiet and the listening to the sounds of nature along the way, perhaps stopping to watch the activities of the chipmunks, an owl, or busy birds. Roger does bike with other friends, but he often goes on his own and describes biking as his meditation.

I asked a friend about her medicine. She loves a fragrant bath at the end of the day. She loves the smell of the bath salts, and the candles that are lit by the tub. (Incense would do the trick as well if that appeals to your senses.) Nice hot water, a luxuriously large bath towel, closing her eyes, and just breathing and relaxing is good for her body and soul, she says.

My friend Jamie says that her medicine is moving her physical body. She loves to run and also practises yoga. She says it clears her mind from stress. As she travels for her work, she has literally run and practised her yoga all over the world!

Joanne, my friend, said that her medicine is to walk by the water (she lives near the ocean). The sights, sounds, and fresh, salty air are rejuvenating to her, particularly when she is also taking along a furry friend. She also finds peace in putzing around her garden: deadheading the flowers, smelling the fresh dirt and blooms, and picking a few edibles for dinner that evening. She also loves music in the background while reading a good novel.

I believe that it is important to partake in your medicine regularly. I recently read a book called *Who Dies* by Stephen and Andrea Levine. The book is about living consciously and also dying consciously from the perspective of a number of different cultures and organized religions.

The authors say that most people's dying days and words are not about what they did in their lives, or what they accumulated in their lives (big house, powerful job, fancy car, bank account, etc.). Most dying words are about the things they *wish* they had done, the dreams that were never pursued and the activities that fell by the wayside in the busyness of day-to-day life—or perhaps about an apology they should have offered or a door that they never opened.

Similarly, it seems to me, are the words you say to a loved one when they are dying. You are not likely going to have a conversation about them wishing they owned a larger house. More likely, it may be about doing something they didn't get around to, like re-visiting a special place or a trip that they always wanted to go on, and kept putting off.

In talking to people about this over the years, a common theme seemed to be about wishing they had had more in-depth conversation with a relative before they passed or a friend they have now lost touch with. I personally wish I had taken more time asking my parents more questions about their lives. My dad had some stories when asked, but Mom was a little less forthcoming on her childhood. During the last years of their lives, I did do more of that, but often now I come up with a question and wonder about their thoughts on the subject.

I don't recall where I heard it, but when you accept death as inevitable, you no longer take your life for granted. Embrace the special moments you have now. I have pondered this many times as I write about joy and my journey.

If you are to live to see the end of today only, what would you regret in your life right now? What are you doing about it? Pay attention. Consider taking the leap and fulfilling that "thing" that you may regret not pursuing.

I am currently embracing my life, and I attempt daily to truly see and hear my surroundings. Feeling fully satisfied with my life is no longer about having a new car, a new house, a new job, or even a fancy trip. Feeling fully satisfied for me at this point is having deep, committed relationships with like-minded people, feeling at peace, smiling at my surroundings, travelling to a place that feels serene, living mindfully, and not paying attention to what others judge or criticize me for. After all, as I said before, what other people think of me is none of my business!

I am working on this book in part as a legacy of life that I want to leave behind when I pass. That could be several decades from now, or it could be next year, or tomorrow. I won't be on my death bed wishing I had listened to the universe about writing about my journey. I even told my husband that if I was to pass before this writing is published, my wish is that he gets the process completed for me.

I was recently listening to a podcast with Kute Blackson. Kute is the amazing, powerfully inspiring author of *You.Are.The.One.* and, more recently, *The Magic of Surrender*. He talked about letting go of people who are no longer a vibrational match for you on your journey. By this I mean, drifting away from those who give you great stress or exhaust you by their attitudes or drama.

I immediately thought of a friend who from my view is in a difficult marriage. I see her being smothered from her own joy and creativity and am sad for that. From the outside, I think she is stuck, but we all have to find our own path. Only we can check out what is happening in our lives and make the choice to either just watch it unfold or to truly see it as it is and consider taking action towards a more meaningful life.

I am convinced that in order to pursue my dreams, I need to surround myself with like-minded people. I often see a vision of a circle of women, discussing their lives with all of its ups and downs. I am constantly turning to a series of Judith Duerk books to inspire that vision, starting with *Circle of Stones*.

This remarkable woman, who recently passed from this world, continues to spark my flame of hope for pure joy and for the people on this planet. She inspires us to ask the question, "How might your life have been different if…?" I am thinking about that and wondering how "our" lives would be different now had we listened years ago to the wisdom of the scientists who warned of global warming and destroying our planet for profit and greed.

I think of the simple lives that people in Bali live and are grateful for. I think of their divine wisdom to pay attention to what is important, and what is simply not that important, like physical possessions and conflict. Every time I visit there, I am reminded of pure joy and the abundance they have that is so different from our North American values.

What is on your bucket list? What are your dreams to be realized during your remaining time on earth? What experiences do you want before you are unable to do them? Where do you want to go? Who do you want to meet? What do you want to do or accomplish? Consider not putting that item on hold once again.

Every time I watch the old movie *The Bucket List* with Morgan Freeman and Jack Nicholson, I am reminded to think about what is on my list. If you haven't seen the movie, it is worth it. Not that I would go sky-diving like they did….

In contrast, what do you want to let go of? What are the things you do out of obligation or habit that don't suit you anymore? What are you doing that used to but no longer brings you joy? What are the relationships in your life that you want to let go of as they cause you nothing but stress, and fill your head with negativity.

I read recently that the Chinese word for "crisis" is the same word for "opportunity". Is that not interesting? I started to think about that and realized I had heard something similar to this before. I am sure you have heard people suggest that when faced with a trying situation or a difficult decision, that there is a lesson to be gathered and learned from it.

My example would be that when I was going through a very stressful divorce, I certainly was not seeing any positive side at the time. But later, I realized that there were positive lessons. The divorce meant that I was now on a different path in my life, and that path could be fabulous. That path taught me to learn to stand up for myself, speak up, and not allow myself to be walked over again. The "crisis" (or opportunity) of a divorce also taught me that I was fully capable of living on my own and taking care of my children and home without a partner. I recall feeling invigorated when I truly saw that.

I have come to believe that our regrets are powerful teachers. I do not want to strive for a life with no regrets. To stop having regrets would suggest that I am not out there really living, but rather staying in a safe cocoon and that my learning has stopped ... a bit boring, right? We are human, and as such, we all make mistakes. Forgive. What did I learn? Let it go. Guess what? It won't be the last mistake you make. I have made more than my share, and I am okay with making more mistakes if it means stretching my mind and perhaps my wisdom.

I truly believe that unless we learn the lesson from a difficult moment, a difficult relationship, a difficult job, etc., we will find ourselves in the same boat over and over again. I heard it said once that life is like a school. We are creatures of habit and tend to hold on to what we are comfortable with, what is "normal" for us. By doing so, we are not growing and expanding on our life's purpose.

Part of starting this journey was that I knew in my heart that I was stuck in my life and so afraid of failure that I wasn't even trying to find a new way. I have learned that it is our ego that keeps us stuck. Our ego fights to protect us from more pain. For example, a little self-talk from my ego: "Don't write a book. You are not capable. If you do write it, there will be those that hate it and will reject you, and that will hurt." The conclusion is that: "I don't want to be hurt, so I will continue living my life safely."

Every day we are faced with decisions, small and large. Learning to trust my initial instincts was difficult, as often I could see an easier way to just go along with the flow, even though my gut was telling me otherwise. I was gradually learning to trust the voice from within, and accepting that if it turns out to be the wrong choice, that's okay.

Not trusting my instincts would mean that I would regret many paths and decisions, and living a life full of regrets is not fun. Repeatedly telling ourselves that we always make the wrong choice doesn't help either. All that does is deepen the hole of despair.

These were some of the learnings as I worked my way through past resentments and difficulties. By at least understanding where I was going wrong, it was becoming clearer which paths to no longer take, and what boundaries needed to be set with some people in my life.

Today when I look back at some of my unhealthy patterns and accept that I was pretending that all was well, I can see that I was caught up in a spiral of repeated patterns. Now I can clearly seen the ways I went wrong by being in victim mode in a number of my primary connections. I now can take full responsibility for my part of the demise of those toxic relationships. I followed this by finally letting them go, so I am free of resentments and anger. I now accept full responsibility for losing myself and allowing others to walk all over me.

With a fuller understanding of my contributions, I am not going back there. There are a couple of toxic relationships that are totally gone from my life, which is fine by me, as I have come out the other side stronger and with clearer boundaries. I will continue to strive to not get backed into a corner with another draining and toxic situation. I no longer grieve those relationships or allow my energy to be consumed by the memories. I have moved on and focus on making the most of every day I have moving forward.

Making decisions on your own is powerful. We all have a degree of inner wisdom. Some of us trust our intuition when making decisions, and some of us are still learning this lesson. The more you trust in yourself, and follow your intuition, the more freedom and joy you will find from within. At least that has been my experience of late. I now know that the sooner I am able to let go of a poor choice, the better off I am in moving forward.

Everyone does not see the world as I do, and that is okay. They just see it differently. For example: Blue is not a better colour than yellow; it is just a different colour. You like blue, and I like yellow.

Find the medicine that you love, not someone's else's idea of the best medicine. Partake in that medicine for you and your own well-being.

Stop acting as if life is a rehearsal,
Live this day as if it were your last.
The past is over and gone.
The future is not guaranteed.
—Wayne Dyer

Sometimes I notice miracles happening around me. I am convinced that they are a result of getting what I focus on. Meghan, my Kundalini teacher has an expression that I love: *Where your attention goes, your energy flows.*

Some time ago, my daughter was having difficulty finding a new apartment. The possibilities were coming up over and over, but would not pan out. After a month or so, I woke up one morning with a calling in my head to participate in a recorded hypnosis meditation. Before I started, my daughter had texted that she was waiting on yet another possibility for a new apartment. As I started the meditation, I set my intention which was for her to find a safe place to live along with her dog. As the hypnosis ended, my phone rang with a text message. She got the apartment! I was so relieved, but also in awe of the timing of the miracle.

The following day, I did another Kundalini practice; the theme of this particular practice was about bringing prosperity into my life.

My intention was to focus on having all of my financial affairs in order. I had made a major investment a few years back and had for months been trying to sell it with no results. So, during the meditation, I put the word out to the universe about finding a buyer and settling this part of my estate. Literally, within the hour of finishing the meditation, I received a call, and I had a buyer.

These are just a couple of miracles that I experienced in the past year and have journaled about. Do I believe? I do. For those who focus on the negative continually and are constantly talking about how "bad things" keep happening, guess what they receive? More of the same.

Living while focusing on what you don't want or have brings more of the same. I know someone who complains about her family, complains about her job, and complains about her lack of energy to do anything. Setting the vision of focusing on what you do want will bring miracles. It takes practise and commitment, but eventually I could see a difference when I changed my approach. It is tough at times, but I keep at it.

I also keep working to block out the negative energy of those around me. I was at a spa a while back, and the spa tech said that my skin was beautiful as it was glowing. She asked what I was doing. I knew why it was glowing: my inner peace was showing through!

The Dalai Lama said once: *"We can never obtain peace in the outer world until we can make peace with ourselves."*

I have learned, that first and foremost, to pour into myself. Pour in love, pour in positive thoughts, pour in peace. Only then can I approach others and show up positively and genuinely. For this reason, I aim to do my meditation and journal work at the beginning of each day to "start off on the right foot", as the expression goes.

There is one last piece of medicine I would like to share. I truly mean it when I say I want to be happy for the rest of my life. Yes, there will be challenges, people moving on, people I love and care for passing on, and other changes happening. I am committed that every time a part of me begins to feel unhappy, I will let the feelings flow through me and then let them go. Depending on the unhappy event, of course, this can take some time—such as grieving a loved one. There is no benefit to me and my life to hold on to a challenge and have it pause my entire day, week, year, or lifetime.

I no longer grieve my parents passing. I miss them being here in human form, and I love them. I know for sure that they are with me in spirit. I feel their guidance all the time. I know that they both lived their lives and gave what they could to their children: guidance, wisdom, or making pastry! I think of them every day, and I am eternally grateful for the wonderful memories.

I continue to talk to them, asking them for guidance by showing me a sign, and I constantly receive from them. I am no longer holding on to the hard memories that got blown up over time. I think of those challenging times, and then let them pass through me as lessons, and I celebrate that I got through them. Period. All that to say, my parents are one of my most effective medicines.

The Eighteenth Stair: ...And Still Climbing

*Surrender to what is.
Let go of what was.
Have faith in what will be.*

—Sonia Ricotti, Canadian Author and Motivational Speaker

The above quote reminds me that all of my struggles, mistakes, poor choices, and traumas in my life are already done. I can not undo the past, and nor should I. Events, people, places, and things of my past have moulded who I am today.

My soul has lived several times over the centuries in other humans before it came to me. My soul will eventually live on in another human on this earth and continue the journey that I continued from others. I have tried to live up to being the best I can be, particularly in this past few years.

I matter.

I am worthy.

I have wisdom and magic to share with the world.

I was told that writing this book would release any self-doubt that this is my path and what I was meant to do in this lifetime. Now that I am near the end of capturing my words and thoughts on paper, I see that clearly.

This writing has allowed me release what is no longer aligned with my values, goals, beliefs, or personal growth. I now trust that what I am doing in this life is truly my pathway. I have found that the more I care for myself, the more I find the courage and strength to grow even more. I am no longer feeling the need for others' approval. I am who I am and trust that what I am doing on this journey is enough.

I know that there will be people in my life who are too afraid to comment on my thoughts here, but I know that perhaps they are listening and taking heed of a nugget or two which in turn may help their journey towards more Joy.

I also know that for some, my growth may activate and stir up some uncomfortable feelings. It is my hope that those who are activated will consider those feelings and question what is really going on inside for themselves.

Perhaps some of this book has sparked thoughts and feelings that have been ignored for a long while, and need action. I also recognize that there are some, who while reading this may see my growth as intimidating, and therefore will respond with silence or distancing.

That is okay.

We all have our own journey, and the contents of this book are pieces of mine. Some may judge me for parts of that journey, but know that I am choosing to ignore that and carry on.

I am choosing kindness for myself and those around me versus being right.

There is a wonderful song that inspired me to start writing called "Legacy of Light" by Fia. She writes her lyrics about taking one day at a time, being grateful, and having a life goal of accomplishing all that she aspires to during this lifetime, leaving nothing undone.

...feeling so blessed to be alive...

...another page in my book...

...I want to know that that I left it all on the table... a legacy of light.

For those still struggling from addiction, I see you. Perseverance and determination to live differently was, and still is my rock. Giving back to those around me is another of my rocks. Learning and nurturing how I now see life is my rock.

But most of all, my rock is living mindfully and taking in every ounce of today. As I have said a number of ways throughout this book: yesterday is already gone, and tomorrow is not yet here, so today is where my focus is.

If addiction is not your journey, we can all strive to live our lives more fully. For those reading this who do not have addiction as an issue, I hope you will find nuggets of inspiration in this writing that will impact how you choose to continue your personal journey.

I choose to live my life as if there is no tomorrow. I recently heard someone say something like: "When you look at people or things differently, people or things look different." Ponder that thought. I did, specifically thinking of a person in my life who I saw as aloof and not caring, but when I look at them now at this point in my journey, I see them as focused on their dreams and ambitions and as someone that I can learn from. I believe that perhaps I was jealous of them living their lives focused on what was right for their journey. I now see that, and it is so freeing.

I am full of Joy for my life and the people around me. I will continue to regularly re-evaluate my goals and ensure that they are aligned with my vision of this more joyous and fulfilling life.

What you think, you become.
What you feel, you attract.
What you imagine, you create.

—Unknown

Say yes to you!

Resources

The following is a list of some of the books that inspired me during my journey:

- Arden, Jann, *If I Knew Then - Finding Wisdom in Failure and Power in Aging*, Random House Canada, 2020
- Arden, Jann, *Feeding my Mother - Comfort and Laughter in the Kitchen as my Mom lives with Memory Loss*, Random House Canada, 2017
- Berger, Ph.D., Allen, *12 Stupid Things That Mess Up Recovery - Avoiding Relapse through Self-Awareness and Right Action*, Hazelden Publishing, Minnesota, USA, 2008
- Blackson, Kute, *You.Are.The.One - A Bold Adventure in Finding Purpose*, Gallery Books, New York, NY, 2016
- Blackson, Kute, *The Magic of Surrender - Finding the Courage to Let Go*, Penguin Random House, New York, NY, 2022
- Carr, Emily, *Sister & I from Victoria to London*, The Royal B.C. Museum, Victoria, B.C., 2011
- Covington, Stephanie S., *A Woman's Way through The Twelve Steps*, Hazelden Publishing, Minnesota, USA, 1994

- Duerk, Judith, *Circle of Stones, A Woman's Journey to Herself,* New World Library, Novato, CA, 2004, 15th Edition
- Duerk, Judith, *I Sit Listening to the Wind, Woman's Encounter Within Herself,* Innisfree Press Inc., Philadelphia, PA, 1993
- Gilbert, Elizabeth, *Big Magic, Creative Living Beyond Fear,* Riverhead Books, New York, NY, 2016
- Johnson, Alex, *Rooms of Their Own—Where Great Writers Write,* Frances Lincoln, UK, 2022
- Kabat-Zinn, Jon, *Mindfulness for Beginners - reclaiming the present moment - and your life,* Sounds True Inc., Boulder, Colorado, 2012
- Knott, Helen, *In My Own Moccasins - A Memoir of Resilience,* University of Regina Press, Saskatchewan, Canada, 2019
- Levine, Stephen & Andrea, *Who Dies?,* Anchor Books, a Division of Random House, Inc. New York, NY, 1982
- Mason-John, Valerie & Groves, Dr. Paramabandhu, *Eight Step Recovery - Using the Buddha's Teachings to Overcome Addiction,* Windhorse Publications, Cambridge, UK, new edition, 2018
- Maté, Gabor, *the Myth of Normal - Trauma, Illness & Healing in a Toxic Culture,* Penguin Random House Canada, Toronto, Ontario, 2022
- Narcotics Anonymous, *Just for Today Daily Meditations,* World Service Office Canada, Mississauga, Ontario, 6th Edition, 1991
- Powell, John, *why am I afraid to tell you who I am?,* Argus Communications Illinois, 1969
- Singer, Michael, *the untethered soul - the journey beyond yourself,* New Harbinger Publications, Oakland, CA, 2007
- Singer, Michael, *The Surrender Experiment,* Yellow Kite Books, UK, 2016
- Singer, Michael, *living untethered - beyond the Human*

RESOURCES

Predicament, New Harbinger Publications, Oakland, CA, 2022

- Thomas-Muller, Clayton, *Life in the City of Dirty Water*, Penguin Random House Canada, 2021
- Tolle, Eckhart, *The Power of Now*, Namaste Publishing, 1st Edition, 1997
- *Vanwynsberghe, Marsha (compiled by), Owning Your Choices - Stories of Courage from 8 Inspirational Women Around the World*, Prominence Publishing, Bolton, Ontario, 2020
- Wiest, Brianna, *The Pivot Year*, Thought Catalog, USA, 2023
- Willowroot, Abby, *Everyday Mindfulness—365 Ways to a Centred Life*, Octopus Publishing Group, London, UK, 2016

REFERENCE

Throughout this writing I refer to my practice of Kundalini yoga and my coach/mentor, Meghan Weir. Here are her credentials:

> Meghan Weir is your Spiritual and Business Catalyst and is obsessed with leading the healing vs. hustling movement.
>
> Meg is known for guiding her clients through deep, transformational work that elicits remembrance of who they are, why they are here, what their magic and medicine is and how to share it with the world.
>
> Through her work, clients drop into their self-sourced power, get out of their way, shed old layers, transmute old programming, and come to a space of deep trust within, where their soul leads, body calibrates, and their mind follows.
>
> Formerly a nurse, Meghan is a Master practitioner in NLP, timeline therapy, hypnotherapy, and rapid resolution therapy. Meg is also a Kundalini yoga and meditation teacher.
>
> She resides on Vancouver Island with her husband and two golden retrievers.
>
> www.meghan-weir.com

Acknowledgements

I sincerely want to thank all those who have supported me on this journey, particularly my family. My husband, Roger, has been a rock for me throughout the entire journey. Thank you, for your love and support. Thank you for your reading, re-reading, editing, and endless hours of listening to my thoughts and dreams while I put these words to paper.

Thank you to my daughters who inspire me to be the best I can be. I love you so much.

Thank you to my dear friend of over forty years, Joanne, for truly hearing me and gently guiding me as I evolve as a more joyful and stronger human being. Your friendship means the world to me. Thank you for reading many of the early drafts and offering your candid and honest feedback.

Thank you also to my relatively new friend, Jamie. I am so grateful to have connected with you a few years ago. I look forward to our weekly check-ins and our candid, unfiltered conversations to keep each other in check and addiction free.

Thank you to Brenda and Jim for your heartfelt support and friendship during my journey. Your encouragement throughout has meant so much to me. Thank you also for the cheerleading throughout my writing of this book.

Thank you to my Chrysalis Group for your feedback and unwavering support. Thank you, Kristina, Jessica, Julie, Marsha, Jolene, and Meg. These are power-house women who have raised the bar in what we can accomplish in life, no matter what our age or status. You all inspired me to write, and you continue to inspire me as I watch your personal journeys.

And finally, I thank the readers of this creation. I wrote this book, first for myself and my own healing, but then for you. It is my wish that you find hope and inspiration to enhance your journey in life. For those still in the early stages of recovery, keep pushing yourself up the stairs. It is well worth the hard work.

Thank you.

Printed in Canada